# 101 ways

## to use your
## first sewing machine

Elizabeth Dubicki

©2006 Elizabeth Dubicki
Published by

**kp krause publications**
*An Imprint of F+W Publications*

**700 East State Street • Iola, WI 54990-0001**
**715-445-2214 • 888-457-2873**

Our toll-free number to place an order or obtain
a free catalog is (800) 258-0929.

The following registered trademark terms and companies appear in this publication:
Baby Lock®, Bernina® of America, Brother®, Chenille by the Inch™, Clotilde®, Fray Check™, Husqvarna® Viking®, Kenmore®, Lycra®, Mod Podge®, Singer®, Velcro®

Library of Congress Catalog Number: 2005934367

ISBN-13: 978-0-89689-309-2
ISBN-10: 0-89689-309-X

Edited by Sarah Brown
Designed by Emily Adler

Printed in China

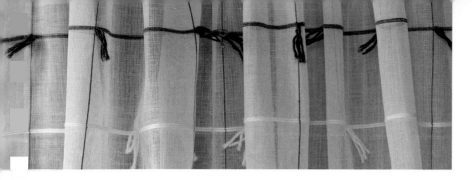

## dedication

To my sister Ellen, with love and appreciation for her creative input and assistance with photography; and to others (some sewers, some not) who lent their first names and inspiration to this book.

## acknowledgments

Machine sewing begins with a machine, and the "first one" photographed herein is a *Bernina activa 240*. I am grateful to Bernina of America for loaning me this dandy powerhouse which I used to make all of the featured projects. If you haven't yet purchased your first machine, here's my advice: Shop and compare the features of the many excellent models on the market today, and buy the best one you can afford from a retailer/dealer who can support your developing skills with one-on-one instruction, service, classes and helpful accessories.

A book needs a publisher, and a writer needs an editor and production team. I am grateful to Krause Publications and the following staff for their efforts: to editor Sarah Brown for planting the seed and helping nurture this project through all phases of production; to photographer Robert Best for wielding lights, cameras, drills, props, wires, etc., with incredible patience and good humor; to illustrator Missy Shepler for deciphering my chicken-scratched drawings; and to designer Emily Adler for making everything look so nice on the printed page.

I must thank, too, the companies who graciously supplied many of the fabrics and notions used in the featured projects. I encourage you to patronize these companies, listed in the Resources on page 188, as their products reflect a sincere dedication to the needs and interests of sewers, and using them will enrich your sewing experience.

Finally, kudos to you, the reader of "101 Ways" for taking your first steps in what I hope will be a lifelong interest in sewing. Trust me, sewing will give you more pleasure and creative rewards than anything you've ever done before! This is one powerful statement coming from me, a lifelong sewer whose first solo garment project (in the early '60s) included setting in a zipper *upside down and backwards*. I've come a long way since then, but I still keep my seam ripper handy. You live, you learn, you rip out and on you sew. Now, let's get started!

# table of contents

chapter 1

# get ready to sew!

# ready to sew!

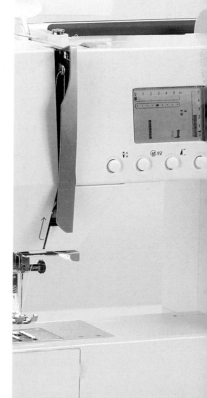

Your first sewing machine ... how thrilling! Unpacking the box, spreading out all of the cool stuff that comes with the machine ... the little bobbins, neat foot attachments. The urge is overwhelming to plug 'er in and zoom away. But, would you drive a car without knowing how to steer it, use the brakes, turn on the lights? Hardly. Before flooring the pedal, read the manufacturer's manual, cover to cover, to understand how your machine operates and become familiar with its nuances. Then, practice, practice, practice.

Along with practice, there are other things you can do to successfully launch your sewing career, such as setting up a sewing area in your home and building a supply of tools, notions and accessories.

# set up your sewing space

Your spouse has a workshop, the kids have a playroom ... you deserve a sewing area. Carve out a sewing niche with electrical outlets, lighting and space for the following:

- ★ Excellent task and ambient lighting (self-explanatory ... who needs eye strain?)

- ★ Sewing table and comfortable chair (to leave your machine "up" and ready to go whenever you need it)

- ★ Cutting table (available for about $100 at any fabric store ... kitchen countertop height ... yeah!)

- ★ Ironing board and steam iron (again, up at all times ... dedicated to sewing ... think kitchen triage: cutting table to sewing machine to ironing board)

- ★ Shelving unit and storage bins to hold folded fabric, notions, trims, patterns, etc.

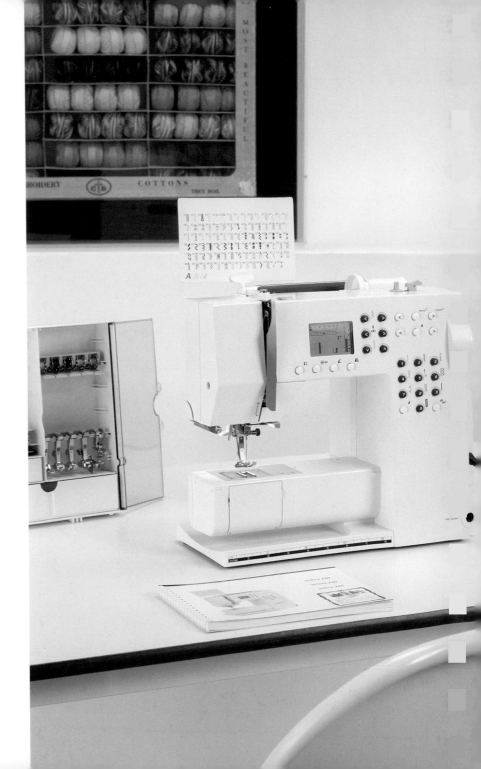

# get the right tools

The machine you've purchased probably comes with some accessories, such as different foot attachments for different stitches, a supply of bobbins, a needle threader, etc. Here are some examples of supplied accessories and others you will need to purchase.

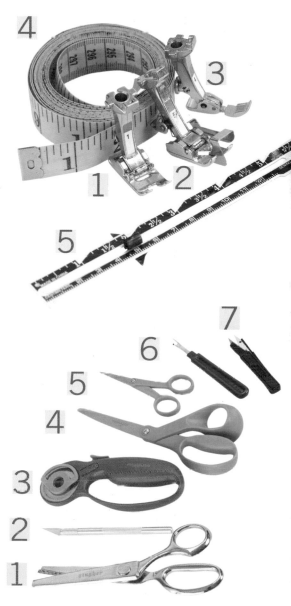

### feet first

The upper right photo shows three foot attachments included with my sewing machine: {1} the *all-purpose foot* is used for basting, straight stitching, zigzag stitching, and some decorative stitching; {2} the *edging foot* with its vertical plate, is used for edgestitching and blind hemming; {3} the *zipper foot* is used to insert zippers, of course, but can also be used to create covered cording and to insert purchased piping, welting, and trims in seams.

### measure twice...

The upper right photo includes: {4} an extra-long 120" tape measure (helpful when making larger décor projects); and {5} the all-important 6" sewing gauge (used for myriad purposes, such as measuring/marking hems and buttonhole placements). In addition to these measuring tools, consider purchasing clear plastic and metal yardsticks, a carpenter's square, a regular tape measure, and a large cutting mat with 1" grid and diagonal/bias cutting guidelines.

### cut once...

With the cutting tools pictured in the lower right photo, you will be equipped to handle most sewing projects, including all of the projects in this book: {1} pinking shears (used to trim seam allowances to prevent raveling, and for creating decorative edges); {2} craft knife (buy a box of replacement blades, too); {3} rotary cutter and replacement blades (excellent for cutting precise fabric strips); {4} bent handle shears (available in left- and right-hand models); {5} small, sharp straight blade scissors (for precise cuts in tight spaces); {6} seam ripper (to efficiently cut hem and seam stitches, and short slits); and {7} thread clipper.

*My cutting tool rule:* Never allow family members to use your cutting tools to cut anything but fabric, thread and sewing notions. Remind them of the scissors, paper, rock hand game: If you catch them using your scissors to cut coupons or wrapping paper, you will hurt their hands with a rock!

# gather notions

Among the hundreds of sewing notions available today, these are the ones I consider to be essential (*coincidentally,* they show up in many of the projects in this book):

* Variety of straight pins

* Safety pins

* Water-soluble fabric marker (buy two!)

* Tailor's chalk

* Fusible seam tape (in varying widths)

* Paper-backed fusible web (in varying weights)

* Fusible interfacing (knit for lightweight fabric; solid for heavier fabrics)

* Thread (all-purpose sewing; rayon embroidery; topstitching; elastic)

* Machine needles (standard, ballpoint, jeans; embroidery)

* Hand sewing needles

* Elastic (cord and wider widths)

* Seam tape

* Hem facing

* Fabric glue

* Spray adhesive

* Polyester fiberfill (always have a bag on hand)

* Quilt batting

* Pillow inserts

* Velcro (hook and loop tape, squares and dots)

* Double-fold bias binding tape

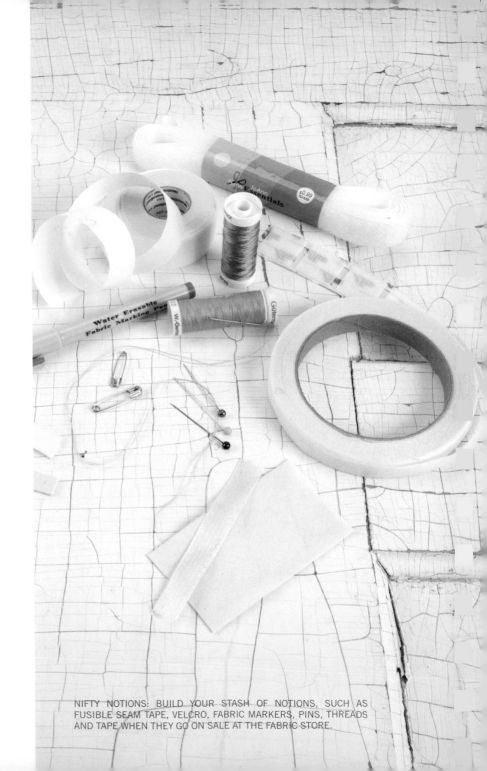

NIFTY NOTIONS: BUILD YOUR STASH OF NOTIONS, SUCH AS FUSIBLE SEAM TAPE, VELCRO, FABRIC MARKERS, PINS, THREADS AND TAPE WHEN THEY GO ON SALE AT THE FABRIC STORE.

# learn basic stitches

Even if your sewing machine doesn't offer decorative stitches, you can still sew up miracles with a few basics, illustrated in the following photos.

## sew on...

Straight and zigzag stitches are basic functions of most home sewing machines. By making adjustments in stitch length and width, you can sew lines of stitches like these: {1} *straight stitches*: used for permanent seams (stitch length set at 10 and 12 stitches per inch), basted seams (stitch length set at 6 to 8 stitches per inch, or other setting prescribed by the machine manufacturer) and gathering lines (no more than 6 stitches per inch); {2} *zigzag stitches*: often used to clean-finish seam allowance raw edges; {3} *satin stitches* (in varying widths): used to make buttonholes, and for decorative purposes, such as outlining appliqués and meant-to-be-seen hems; {4} examples of machine-programmed *buttonholes*; {5} machine-programmed *eyelet buttonhole* (an option on some machines); {6} *triple stitches* (an option on some machines): used for decorative and functional purposes on denim and jeans projects.

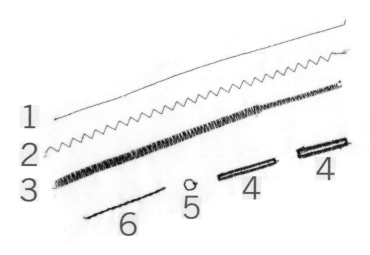

## and sew forth...

Versatile straight and zigzag stitches not only sew fabrics together, they can be used to attach other materials to a project. Here are some examples: {1} *zigzag stitches* used to attach buttons; {2} *bar tacking* (essentially a tight zigzag stitch), often used as a decorative reinforcement of a stress point, such as the upper corners of patch pockets and the upper edge of a slit seam; {3} *bar tacking* used to attach rings and buckles; {4} *straight stitches* stitched extra close to piping trim, using the zipper foot attachment; {5} *straight stitches* used to attach ribbon trim, with neat edgestitching accomplished with the edging foot attachment).

Long ago and far away, sewing was taught in junior high, and girls were introduced to the home economics of this craft by making an apron. An apron?! Who wears that anymore? What I *do* wear is my self-designed sewer's tool belt with plenty of pockets to hold my scissors, fabric marker, tape measure and other items. This one-size-fits-most belt serves as a get-you-started project and tutorial for other projects in this book. *Note:* Review the Basic Sewing instructions beginning on page 175 before starting this project for basic instructions and for explanations of terms like "edgestitching," "topstitching" and "clean-finish."

make your first project: sewer's tool belt

## materials

[materials annotation] Essential materials are listed to make the featured project, such as specific yardage in a specific width, required notions and other unique materials. Not listed are standard sewing supplies, such as thread, sewing machine, sewing needles, and measuring, marking and cutting tools.

★ 1 yd. medium-weight cotton or cotton/blend fabric

[fabric annotation] If the fabric width is not noted, a 45"- or 54"-wide or wider fabric will be adequate for the project.

★ 2 yd. purchased sew-in piping in coordinating color

[annotation] You choose the fabric; therefore, you select the coordinating color of purchased piping, which is available prepackaged or by-the-yard in most fabric stores.

## cutting instructions

From the cotton fabric, cut:
- Two 30" x 15" pocket panels
- One 36" x 2" tie strip

[cutting instructions annotation] Measurements are given width x length and correspond to the fabric width (selvage to selvage) x fabric length, unless otherwise noted. Therefore, you are to cut two 30"-wide panels across the fabric width that are each 15" long (hereafter referred to as the "pocket panels"). You are also to measure and cut one 2"-deep x 36"-long strip, also across the fabric width (hereafter referred to as the "tie strip").

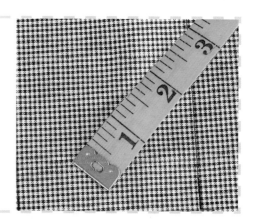

# *instructions*

[instructions annotation] Unless otherwise noted, you will sew all fabrics right sides together using a ⅝" seam allowance for garment projects and a ½" seam allowance for non-garment and decor projects. If stitching two layers, create machine knots with backstitches at the beginning and end of each stitched seam.

**1** Use your zipper foot to baste a length of piping to each long edge of one pocket panel.

**2** Stitch the pocket panels together, leaving one short edge unstitched. Trim the seams and corners, and turn right-side out. Fold under the seam allowances on the panel open edges and slipstitch the opening closed. Press the seams flat.

[step 2 annotation] Sew the panels right sides together, using ½" seams, around three sides, pivoting at the corners. "Leaving one short edge open" means do not stitch one 15"-long edge of the pocket panels. "Trim seams and corners" means to cut about ¼" from the seam allowances and to diagonally trim the corner seam allowances. "Turn right-side out" means pulling the fabric through the panel unstitched edges so that the right side of the fabric faces outward and the wrong side of the fabric, as well as the seams, are hidden inside the panel layers. "Fold under the seam allowances ... and slipstitched closed" means turning under ½" on the opening raw edges, pinning these edges so that their folds are aligned, and using a needle and thread to slipstitch the edges together by hand to close the opening. "Press the seams flat" means manipulating the stitched seams to remove all creases, folds and wrinkles before pressing the seams flat.

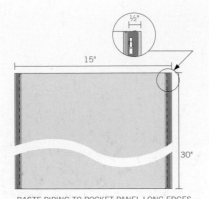

½"

15"

30"

BASTE PIPING TO POCKET PANEL LONG EDGES.

**1**

[illustration annotation] The right side of fabric is shaded; the wrong side is not.

*sewer's tool belt sewer's tool belt sewer's tool be*

**3** With piped edges at top and bottom, fold the panel lower edge upward to create a 6"-deep pocket area. Measure and topstitch the pocket lines, perpendicular to the panel lower edge fold, and edgestitch the panel side edges, as shown.

[step 3 annotation] Follow the measurements in the illustration and use a water-soluble fabric marker to mark the vertical pocket lines, and then stitch them through all layers; also edgestitch the pocket panel side edges, through all layers, to close them.

**4** Press under ½" on each tie strip edge. Fold the strip in half widthwise and wrong sides together, and edgestitch all edges. Cut the strip into two 17½"-long ties. Stitch a tie cut end to each pocket panel upper back edge corner, as shown.

[step 4 annotation] Press under the ½" seam allowance on all strip edges, fold the strip in half and stitch the folded edges to create a double-layer edgestitched tie. The illustration shows where and how to topstitch the tie cut ends to the upper back corners of the pocket panel.

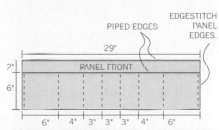

FOLD PANEL TO CREATE POCKETS. EDGESTITCH THE SIDE EDGES AND TOPSTITCH AS SHOWN TO FORM POCKETS.

**3**

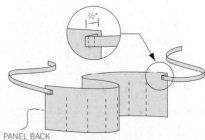

PANEL BACK

FOLD UNDER ½" AND STITCH THE TIE ENDS TO POCKET PANEL UPPER BACK CORNERS.

**4**

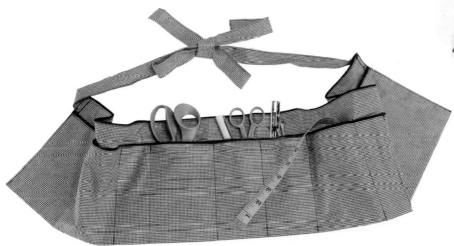

# updated garments

Here are easy and creative techniques for repairing, altering and updating your wardrobe with the help of a sewing machine. The happy outcome is that you will get more mileage out of the clothes you own. This means more money in your pocket to spend in other ways (like on fabric at the next big sale).

# mending a ripped seam

As long as it's just the seam that's ripped — and not the garment fabric itself — this is an easy repair. Simply re-stitch the seam on its original line. I begin and end my repair seam about 1" above and 1" below the intact seam stitches, and machine-knot with backstitches at both ends. This bit of overlap is my insurance policy against a future rip.

# replacing buttons

Sewing buttons by hand is *not* my favorite activity (nor yours, I suspect). You're in luck because your machine can take over this task. Use my technique (or the one recommended by your sewing machine manufacturer), which also works to attach D-ring buckles, plastic rings used in curtain and shade projects, and other decorative objects small enough to fit under the foot and within your machine's maximum zigzag stitch width.

1 For buttons and plastic rings, select the zigzag stitch and attach the appropriate foot. Adjust the stitch length to zero. Position the button on the fabric, slide both under the needle and lower the foot.

2 Manually lower the needle into one buttonhole and take a stitch (zig). Repeat to determine where the needle hits the opposite buttonhole in the next stitch, and adjust the stitch width until the needle enters this hole (zag).

3 Now that the exact stitch width has been set, press the pedal and let the machine do its job to stitch the button, taking 10 to 12 zigzag stitches between the holes.

4 For a four-hole button, stitch the first two holes diagonally. Then, rotate the button/fabric a quarter turn, and stitch the remaining two holes to form an X.

5 To attach a D-ring buckle, like those used on the jeans pocket on page 31 and skirt featured on page 34, follow the above steps, but set the stitch length slightly above zero. As you zigzag stitch over the buckle, apply gentle pressure with your fingers to help move the ring under the needle. *Note:* Too much pressure might break the needle; too little pressure may create a thread jam or ridge. You will learn how much pressure to apply with practice.

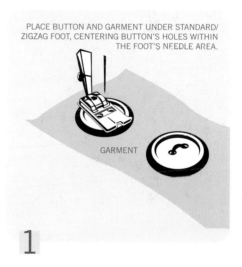

PLACE BUTTON AND GARMENT UNDER STANDARD/ ZIGZAG FOOT, CENTERING BUTTON'S HOLES WITHIN THE FOOT'S NEEDLE AREA.

GARMENT

1

# shortening a skirt

Love the skirt, but hate its dowdy length? Shorten it by measuring, cutting off the excess skirt, finishing the cut edge, and finally hand sewing or machine stitching the new hem. There are two general skirt hems — *folded* and *topstitched*. When shortening a purchased skirt, replicate the original hem style (folded or topstitched) and maintain the original hem depth. *Note:* This purchased skirt has a topstitched hem.

## general materials (for any hemming project)

* Sewing gauge
* Tailor's chalk
* Straight pins
* Coordinating seam tape (available in the notions section of any fabric store)
* Matching sewing thread
* Sewing needle (optional)

## folded hem

**1** Try on the skirt with the shoes you intend to wear with it. Fold under and pin the hem at the center front and check the length in a full-length mirror. Adjust up or down until you're satisfied with the new length, and then take off the skirt, being careful not to disturb the pins.

**2** Use tailor's chalk to mark the fold of the new hemline on the skirt right side, and remove the pins. Set the sewing gauge at the distance from the original hem fold to the new hemline mark, and mark the shortened hemline around the entire skirt on the right side. Fold under and pin the skirt on the marked line, try on the skirt again, and make any desired adjustments until you're satisfied with the length.

**3** Set your sewing gauge at the depth of the existing hem. Measure and mark this distance *down from the newly marked hemline* and around the entire skirt; this is the trimming line. (*Note:* If you're taking up less than the full depth of the existing hem, clip the hem stitches and unfold the hem to mark this trimming line.) Trim the excess skirt length on the marked line.

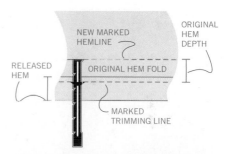

NEW MARKED HEMLINE

ORIGINAL HEM DEPTH

RELEASED HEM

ORIGINAL HEM FOLD

MARKED TRIMMING LINE

MARK TRIMMING LINE WITH SEWING GAUGE SET AT ORIGINAL HEM DEPTH, RELEASING EXISTING HEM IF NECESSARY.

**1**

**4** Refer to the Sewing and Finishing Seams instructions on page 177 to clean-finish the hem cut edge. Stitch seam tape over the hem right side, allowing about ¼" of tape to extend beyond its edge.

**5** Fold up the hem on the marked line and press. *Note:* To prevent a ridge from hem tape showing through on the skirt right side when pressing, slide a piece of cardboard between the hem upper edge and the skirt as you press.

**6** Slipstitch the hem by hand, catching just the tape upper edge in your stitches; or, if your machine is appropriately equipped, refer to the manual to blindstitch the hem.

OPENED, THE HEM REVEALS ITS CLEAN-FINISHED EDGE AND HEM TAPE THAT EXTENDS APPROXIMATELY ¼" BEYOND THE CUT EDGE.

CLOSED AND WITH ITS LOWER EDGE FOLD ALREADY PRESSED, THE HEM IS NOW READY TO BE SLIPSTITCHED BY HAND.

# topstitched hem

**1** Follow the Folded Hem instructions Steps 1, 2 and 3 on page 21 to measure, mark and trim the excess skirt length with this important exception. **Make sure to *double the depth* of the existing hem** as you measure down from the new hemline to mark the trimming line.

**2** Fold and press the hem on its new hemline. Fold under half the hem depth and press again. Topstitch the hem close to the inner fold.

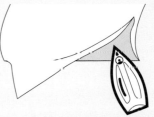

FOLD AND PRESS THE FULL DEPTH OF THE HEM.

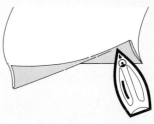

FOLD UNDER HALF THE HEM DEPTH AND PRESS AGAIN.

**2**

## about linings

Skirt and pant linings are shorter than and often unattached to the outer fabric. If there is no chance that the lining will peek out under the outer fabric's newly shortened hem, leave the lining as is. A dramatic shortening, however, means you'll need to shorten the lining, too. In this event, follow the Topstitched Hem instructions to shorten the lining exactly as much as you've shortened the garment hem. Doing this assures that the outer fabric and lining will retain their lengths in proportion to each other.

# *shortening dress pants*

Follow the Folded Hem instructions on page 21 with the following exceptions to Steps 1 and 2:

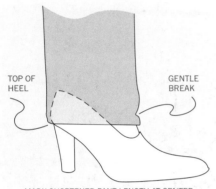

TOP OF HEEL

GENTLE BREAK

MARK SHORTENED PANT LENGTH AT CENTER FRONT AND BACK.

**1**

**1** Ask a friend to help you pin and mark each pant leg separately. Why? Take your cue from Mary, who has one leg that's about ½" shorter than the other. This means that each leg of every pair of pants she buys must be marked individually before shortening, otherwise they will be uneven. It's entirely likely that you, too, have slightly uneven legs, so pin each pant hem and compare.

**2** Make sure to allow enough pant length in front for a gentle break (fold) over the top of your foot, and enough length in back to end at the top of your shoe heel. Make a chalk mark at the pinned hemline folds, front and back. Mark the new hemline by using a ruler to draw a line between these marks. The resulting hemline may slant down from front to back, but that's ok. Your pants have been marked to fit you, and that's the whole point, isn't it?

lengthening a skirt or dress pants

To lengthen a skirt or pair of pants with a folded hem, first determine whether it's possible to iron out the existing hemline crease. Susan suggests dabbing full strength white vinegar on the crease before steam pressing. If your home pressing efforts fail, ask your dry cleaner to press out the crease. Follow these steps to lengthen a garment using packaged hem facing, available in the notions section of any fabric store.

**1** Clip the hem stitches and open the hem so that it lays flat. Determine the desired amount of extra length and set this measurement on your sewing gauge. Mark this distance down from the hem crease and around the entire garment on its right side.

**2** Trim the excess hem ½" beyond on this marked line and clean-finish the cut edge.

**3** Follow the Folded Hem Step 4 instructions on page 22 and refer to the photos below to stitch the hem facing to the hem edge about ⅛" to ¼" below the newly marked hemline. Follow the Folded Hem Step 5 and 6 instructions to finish the hem.

HEM OPEN (LEFT) AND CLOSED (RIGHT) ILLUSTRATE THE EXTRA INCHES IN LENGTH PROVIDED BY A HEM FACING.

# letting out and taking in

Some fitting issues can be corrected by letting out or taking in a garment's existing seams. It's amazing what a difference small seam adjustments can make in the look and wearing comfort of your clothes.

# letting out

When letting out, don't just concentrate on the precise area where the garment is snug (for example, that irritating spot at your upper thighs), as letting out a small section of a seam may create an awkward "bubble." Try my technique for "easing the squeeze" of your garments:

**1** Try on the garment and pin-mark the upper and lower points on each side seam (and center front and center back seams, if possible) where it's tight. Take off the garment and transfer these marks to the inside seams.

**2** For each seam, use tailor's chalk to draw a stitching line that begins approximately 2" above the upper mark, gradually eases *into the existing seam allowance*, and then back to the original seam at least 2" below the lower mark. *Note:* For some garments, you may decide to let out the entire seam, in which case, you must clip and release enough of the hem to allow for this.

**3** Baste the seams on the marked lines, and then clip the original seam stitches between the beginning and ending points of the basted stitches.

**4** Try on the garment to assess the fit and make any desired adjustments. Once you are satisfied, stitch the new seams, stitching over the original seam stitches at the beginning and end, or making a machine knot with back stitches at the end if altering the entire seam.

**5** Remove the basting stitches and press the eased seams open. *Note:* If you let out the entire seam, you will now need to re-stitch the hem.

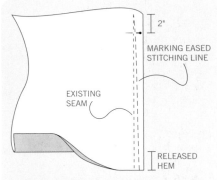

2"

MARKING EASED
STITCHING LINE

EXISTING
SEAM

RELEASED
HEM

BEGIN AT LEAST 2" ABOVE PIN-MARK TO DRAW AN
EASED STITCHING LINE.

2

# taking in

The technique of *taking in* is similar to *letting out*, so review the letting out information on page 28 before following these instructions.

**1** Try on the garment and mark the upper points on the seams where the fit begins to be loose. If adjusting side seams, take equal size tucks in each seam and pin them. Take off the garment and transfer these marks to the inside seams.

**2** For each seam, use tailor's chalk to draw a stitching line that begins approximately 2" above the marked upper point, gradually eases *into the garment*, continues down the seam in accordance with the marks, and eases back to the original seam stitches 2" below the lower mark. *Note:* If fit is not an issue, you may want to take in the entire length of the seams in question. In this case, you must clip and release enough of the hem to allow for this.

**3** Baste the seams on the marked lines, and try on the garment to assess the fit. After making any desired adjustments, stitch the new seams, stitching over the original seams at the beginning and ending points, or a making a machine knot with back stitches at the end if you re-stitch an entire seam.

**4** Remove the basting and the original seam stitches between the beginning and ending points of the new seam. Trim the seam allowances in the altered areas so that they are even with the original seam allowances, and clean-finish the cut edges. Press the new seam open. *Note:* If you let out the entire seam, you will now need to re-stitch the hem.

**5** Unless the alteration is minimal and the lining doesn't appear bunchy, follow the above instructions to take in the garment lining at corresponding seams.

TAKE IN EQUAL AMOUNTS AT SIDE SEAMS.

1

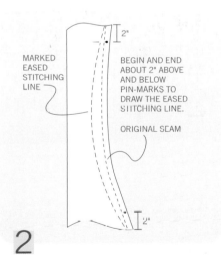

MARKED EASED STITCHING LINE

2"

BEGIN AND END ABOUT 2" ABOVE AND BELOW PIN-MARKS TO DRAW THE EASED STITCHING LINE.

ORIGINAL SEAM

2"

2

good jeans

"Do you know the difference between $50 jeans and $200 jeans?" Martha asked. "Distressed fabric? The sling of the hip? The designer's moniker?" I replied. "Nope," she said. "It's all about the pockets." My observant girl was right — the more embellished the rear pockets, the more costly the retail jeans. So, I loaded up my bobbins and took some of Martha's favorite denims for a walk on the wild side. Her response ("Good jeans, Ma!") has helped conserve her wardrobe budget, while warming my thrifty soul.

# pick your pocket

Before you can embellish a pocket, you must remove it from the jeans. This takes about 10 minutes with the aid of a seam ripper. Pick out all extraneous threads, open the pocket side and lower edge seam allowances, and press flat.

To reattach the embellished pocket, turn under the seam allowances on their original foldlines and press on the wrong side. Apply fusible seam tape underneath the pocket edges, fuse the pocket to the jeans in its original position, and topstitch around the side and lower edges; re-stitch any bar tacking that appeared on the original pocket, too. Here are a few pocket ideas to inspire your own creations ... take your pick.

## tex-mex primer

Here's what happens when you dump a stash of rayon thread on the sewing table and experiment with your machine's decorative stitch offerings. This mixed-up mash of colorful stitchery has a south-of-the-border look, don't you think?

## ellie mae

Hearts never seem to go out of style. I cut this slightly askew version from scrap fabric, fused it to the pocket and then satin stitched the edges. The interior squiggly lines make it a bit more abstract, as do the metal button accents.

## on the slant

Decorative stitches, radiating from upper left to lower right, make up this pocket design. Martha says the satin-stitched D-ring is a perfect hook for her sunglasses. (And I thought it was just for fun!)

## fresh-picked crops

Sometimes jeans grow in reverse ... the longer we wear them, the shorter they get. When this happens, it's time to crop them.

1   Use your sewing gauge and tailor's chalk to mark 4"-5" up from the original hem on each jeans leg and around the leg circumference. Trim each leg on the marked line and zigzag the cut edges.

2   Apply fusible seam tape to the wrong side of each leg over the zigzag stitches.

3   Mark a 2"-3"-deep hem on each leg; fold and press the hem on the marked line, then fuse the hem upper edge.

4   On the right side of each pant leg, stitch two rows of parallel decorative stitches around each pant leg, the first aligned with the hem upper edge and the second just below it.

5   If you miss the distressed or frayed edges of the original jeans, scrub the hems with sandpaper. After a few washings, the fabric should begin to fray again.

A DOUBLE ROW OF DECORATIVE STITCHES NOT ONLY LOOKS GOOD, BUT ALSO COVERS THE INSIDE HEM EDGE TO PREVENT FRAYING.

# denim detailing

The little jean skirt is a wardrobe must-have, but every skirt needs an upgrade once in a while. This decorative trim from Expo International (see the Resources on page 188) does the job at the back yoke and around the hem. Use fusible seam tape underneath the trim and decorative topstitching at the trim upper edge to keep it in place. The D-ring, attached at the top of the back slit with satin stitches, is both decorative and functional as it protects this vulnerable seam against a nasty rip.

Bouclé suit fabric and denim make a brilliant combination. I love the contrast of nubby, loosely woven bouclé and its soft fringe against the rugged texture of sturdy denim. Here's how to replicate this undercollar and fringe on your jean jacket.

collar-ful fringe

ANY LOOSELY WOVEN FABRIC CAN BECOME UNIQUE FRINGE. THE UPPER SAMPLE WAS MADE FROM THE FEATURED BOUCLÉ AND THE LOWER SAMPLE WAS MADE FROM A MORE FINELY WOVEN SOLID.

## materials

★ Jean jacket with collar
★ ¼ yd. loosely woven bouclé or tweed fabric
★ ¼ yd. heavy-weight fusible web
★ Topstitching or embroidery thread

## instructions

1. Place the undercollar of your jacket over the paper side of the fusible web. Trace around the collar outer edges. Remove the collar and draw the lower edge of the tracing to replicate the collar lower edge seam. Cut out this collar shape.

2. Fuse the cutout to the wrong side of the bouclé fabric. Cut the fabric flush with the cutout lower edge, but cut the fabric about ½" beyond the cutout side and upper edges. Remove the web paper backing and fuse the bouclé to the jacket undercollar, allowing the excess unfused fabric to extend beyond the collar side and upper edges.

3. To make the fringe, cut a 2"-wide strip of bouclé that's long enough to cover the collar side and upper edges. Fold the strip in half widthwise and stitch the length of the strip ⅜" from the fold. Clip the fold to open the strip, and press it flat.

4. With the opened strip edge aligned with the excess undercollar fabric, pin the strip around the upper collar side and upper edges. Satin stitch the strip to the collar at the strip center. Also, satin stitch the collar lower edge just above the collar seam.

5. Pull the threads on the strip edges and on the excess fabric of the bouclé undercollar to create the fringe.

◁ THE SATIN STITCHES THAT EDGE THE UPPERCOLLAR ALSO PREVENT THE BOUCLÉ FROM FRAYING AT THE UNDERCOLLAR EDGES.

# denim and decorative stitching

Experiment with your machine's decorative stitches, including the satin stitch, before working a design on jeans or other non-denim garment. Here are my tips and others offered by my sewing colleagues, Jo and Annette.

* Your machine manufacturer will tell you to use a needle that's appropriate for the fabric you're sewing. **Do not ignore this, especially for denim.** Select a needle that's identified as "denim" or "jeans," and start your project with a new one. Replace it with a fresh needle when you sense it's getting dull.

* For topstitching and edgestitching thick pockets, plackets, collars, etc., Jo suggests using a piping foot. "The bulky edge fits nicely under the right side of the foot, making it easy to stitch very close to an edge without 'falling off,'" she says. Jo also recommends a slightly longer-than-usual straight stitch and jeans topstitching thread (available from several thread companies) for undetectable reattachment of an embellished jeans pocket.

* Decorative stitching uses lots of thread. If you wind an extra bobbin or two before you start stitching, you will save time. Also, before stitching a critical row, make sure you have enough bobbin thread ... then you won't have to worry about matching the stitch pattern where you left off if your bobbin runs dry.

* To conserve your supply of rayon embroidery thread, use it in the needle only and a denim-colored all-purpose thread in the bobbin. Who's going to see inside the pocket anyway?

* For pockets, start and end stitching lines, whenever possible, within seam allowances. Your artistic design will "fill the canvas," making you (and your grade school art teacher) very happy with the results.

* Do not place a hot iron directly on decorative rayon stitches, says Annette, as it will flatten the stitches and possibly weaken the thread.

* If your machine has embroidery functions, Jo recommends placing a layer of water-soluble stabilizer on top of the fabric before stitching. The stabilizer prevents the embroidery stitches from sinking between the yarns of the fabric. A quick "bath" removes the excess stabilizer, leaving just the embroidery threads on the surface.

* For stitching over thick denim seams, your machine manufacturer may provide a height compensation tool. The ones I've seen are basically a stack of plastic shims, connected at one end with a grommet. Placing a shim or shims under the outer edge of the presser foot will help it "ride" over the thickest part of a jeans seam. Check the notions section of a fabric store for such a tool if your machine doesn't come equipped with it.

Too low ... too high. If the "V" of your "T" isn't right, try altering it with these easy techniques.

*Ts for two*

# lace insert

For this tangerine tee, the "V" is filled with a piece of lace. To add similar filler, cut the desired depth of lace and adhere it to the underside of the neckline band with fusible seam tape. Trim the excess lace, as necessary, but make sure the lace edges extend about ¼" beyond the band seam. To secure the lace, topstitch the entire neckline band seam with matching thread, catching the lace edges in the stitching. *Note:* Instead of lace, consider using a section of crochet trim purchased by the yard, salvaged from another garment or recycled from vintage tea towels or other linens.

# vertical gathers

This periwinkle tee now features vertical gathers that change its style from plain to trendy with a better bodice fit. The gathers are created with a 2" length of elastic cord. To attach the elastic and create the gathers:

**1** Turn the T-shirt inside out and mark the elastic placement by drawing a 3"-3½" vertical line from the V point down the shirt center.

**2** Machine-tack one end of the elastic cord at each end of this line.

**3** Set your machine for a zigzag stitch that's wide enough to cover the elastic cord (but not pierce it). Insert the needle to one side of the cord at its upper edge. Lower the presser foot.

**4** Stretch the elastic (but not the shirt) to cover the marked line and zigzag over it, being careful not to catch the elastic in your needle.

**5** Release the elastic and the gathers appear!

A LITTLE BIT OF LACE AND A LENGTH OF ELASTIC CORD MAKE ALL THE DIFFERENCE IN THESE NECKLINES.

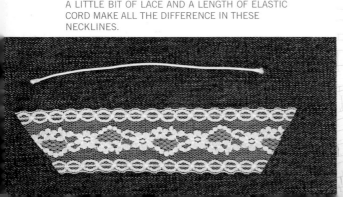

old suit / new suit

## cuffs

If the silk tweed fabric of last year's suit jacket still looks contemporary, but its style is dated, you can update its look by shortening the jacket sleeves and giving them 2½"-deep folded hems and turned-back cuffs. Clip about 2" on each sleeve seam for vents, and topstitch around the vents and the sleeve lower edges. With a new sleeve length and cuffs, the jacket now looks more in step with today's fashion.

THE CONTRAST BETWEEN TRADITIONAL TWEED AND ORGANZA RUFFLES MAKES THIS SKIRT MORE INTERESTING.

SHORTENED SLEEVES AND TURNED BACK CUFFS GIVE THIS TRADITIONAL JACKET A TRENDIER LOOK.

## flirty skirt

Add an ounce of flirty flounce at a skirt lower edge with gathered 1½"-wide organza ribbon; see the Gathering instructions in Machine Stitches on page 176. (*Note:* To determine the ribbon yardage for a skirt ruffle, measure the skirt's lower edge circumference and multiply by 1.5.) Topstitch the ribbon's gathered edge to the hem underside so that 1" of ribbon peeks out, creating the illusion of a petticoat.

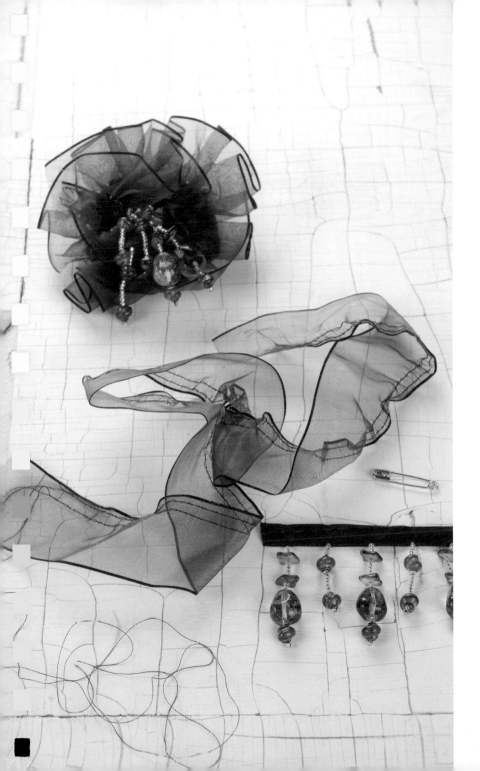

## ribbon pin

The ribbon that adds the lower edge ruffle to the skirt suit at left also makes a nice lapel pin. To make a similar pin, machine baste and gather 1 yard of 1½"-wide sheer ribbon to measure 12"; knot the basting threads and trim the excess thread. Cut a 2½"-diameter circular pin backing from a heavy-weight fabric (such as two layers of fused denim). Starting in the backing center, use fabric glue to glue the ribbon gathered edge in a spiral to completely cover the backing. Fold and glue the header of a 3" length of beaded trim to create a cluster, and glue the header to the center of the ribbon spiral. Use a safety pin to attach your ribbon creation to a jacket lapel.

If you think buttonholes are just for buttons, think again. This blah, white-on-white cotton/Lycra dress needed a color boost and some eye catching detail. Buttery soft, powder blue lambskin salvaged from a worn jacket provided the color, and machine made buttonholes around the hem band added the visual interest.

To replicate this look on a dress or skirt, stitch an even number of evenly spaced vertical buttonholes around the garment lower edge. Cut strips of leather (faux suede or other fabric that won't fray at its cut edges) with pinking shears. Weave the strips through the buttonholes, overlapping and gluing the ends, as necessary, inside the garment.

To make the belt below, use 1"-wide belt webbing (available by the yard and in belt making kits) and a pair of purchased decorative rings for the buckle. Follow the manufacturer's instructions to cover the webbing with a strip of leather and edgestitch the sides (using a leather needle, of course). Then, use Velcro squares or dots to secure the belt end that's looped through the buckle rings.

◁ YOU DON'T HAVE TO MAKE THE BELT, BUT YOU CAN MAKE A PURCHASED ONE BETTER! WITH ITS CONVENIENT PRE-CUT SLITS, THIS BELT WAS AN IDEAL CANDIDATE FOR WOVEN LEATHER ACCENTS, TOO.

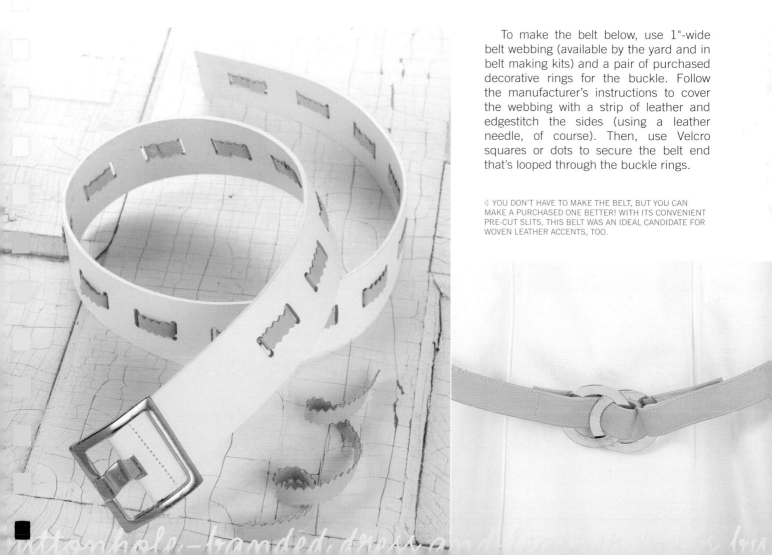

buttonhole-banded dress

Waistbands are out and dropped waists are in. To improve a skirt that's "waisting away" in your closet, take a seam ripper to its waistband and remodel it, following this process.

drop-waist skirt with sash

## materials

* Skirt with waistband and plain zipper closure
* Lightweight fusible knit interfacing
* 1"-wide matching grosgrain ribbon in length equal to the skirt waist circumference, plus 3"
* ¼ yd. lightweight coordinating fabric for the sash, such as georgette, crepe de chine or dupioni

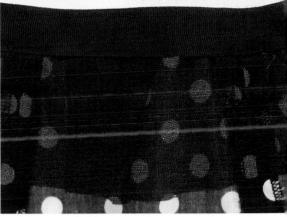

FUSED INTERFACING STABILIZES THE SKIRT UPPER EDGE, AND GROSGRAIN RIBBON SERVES AS THE FACING FOR ITS NEW NO-WAISTBAND STYLE.

## instructions

**1** Use your seam ripper to carefully remove the skirt waistband; set the waistband aside.

**2** To stabilize the waist raw edge, cut and fuse a band of lightweight knit interfacing to the wrong side of the skirt upper edge. *Note:* While this is not the traditional application for fusible interfacing (normally applied to individual pieces of a garment before they're sewn together), it worked well for this waist re-do.

**3** Stitch the ribbon to the waist right side, folding under ½" on the ribbon ends and butting these folds to the skirt closure edges. Fold the ribbon to the skirt inside and press. Edgestitch the waist upper folded edge, stitching over the ribbon as shown.

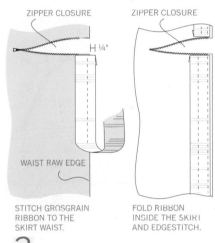

STITCH GROSGRAIN RIBBON TO THE SKIRT WAIST.

FOLD RIBBON INSIDE THE SKIRT AND EDGESTITCH.

**3**

**4** Now, back to the waistband. Cut the waistband into 1½" lengths for sash loops. Press under ¼" on each loop raw edge. Determine the number of desired loops (the featured skirt has seven loops, with each positioned over a skirt seam) and edgestitch the loops around the skirt approximately ½" below the waist folded edge.

**5** Fold the sash fabric in half widthwise and stitch one short edge and the long edge. Turn the sash right-side out, fold under the seam allowance on the open edge and edgestitch.

**6** Thread the sash through the loops and tie the sash at a side seam.

One black satin shawl is great, but two are better! I found this pair of shawls at a discount clothing retailer for $10 each. By simply stitching them together at their long edges — and leaving about 14" unstitched at the center of this seam for the head opening — the two shawls became one luxuriously fringed evening wrap. How easy is that?

*evening poncho*

This one piece wraparound robe (with optional straps) can be your very first made-from-scratch wearable. It's a one-size-fits-most project that everyone in your family will want after they see how comfy and practical yours is.

*bath wraps*

★ 1 yd. 60"-wide velour fabric

★ 1 yd. ¾"-wide elastic

★ 2 pairs of sew-in Velcro squares

*instructions*

**1** Cut a 32"-long panel across the width of the fabric. Wrap the panel around your upper body above the bust like a towel, overlapping the excess fabric in the front. Determine how much fabric to trim from the panel width, depending on how much ease you desire at the hips. Trim the panel and set the trimmed piece aside.

**2** Fold under and topstitch 1"-deep hems at the panel side edges, and a 1"-deep hem at the panel lower edge.

**3** To create the upper edge elastic casing, fold under 2½" and topstitch two parallel lines, the first ½" from the casing inner edge and the second ½" from the casing fold.

**4** Thread the elastic through one casing opening with a bodkin or large safety pin. Pin one elastic end flush with a casing opening. Wrap the robe around you, again overlapping the edges in front as desired, and pull the elastic to create the desired fit; pin the elastic at the second casing opening and trim the excess.

**5** Edgestitch the casing openings twice to close them and to secure the elastic.

**6** To add the optional straps, cut two 2" x 18" strips, fold each in half widthwise and stitch the long edges. Turn each strap right-side out and press. Fold under ½" on the strap open ends and edgestitch them closed.

**7** On the casing wrong side, pin the strap ends at the points where the wrap overlaps. Stitch the strap ends over the original casing stitches. Determine the desired positions of the straps in back, and repeat.

**8** Separate the Velcro sections and stitch sections to the casing right and wrong sides, as appropriate, to secure the front overlapped closure.

OPEN, THE BATH WRAP REVEALS ITS ONE-PIECE CONSTRUCTION WITH OPTIONAL SHOULDER STRAPS.

# better bath and boudoir

enjoyable as possible. They can be if you're surrounded with pretty fabrications. From a female perspective, the hours spent in the bathroom washing, waxing, shaving, styling, plucking, powdering, curling and primping should be as enjoyable as possible. They can be if you're surrounded with pretty fabrications. From a female perspective, the hours spent in the bathroom washing, waxing, shaving, styling, plucking, powdering and primping should be as enjoyable as possible. They can be if you're surrounded with pretty fabrications. From a female perspective, the hours spent in the bathroom washing, waxing, shaving, styling, plucking, powdering, curling and primping should be as enjoyable as possible. They can be if you're surrounded with pretty fabrications. From a female perspective, the hours spent in the bathroom washing, waxing, shaving, styling, plucking, powdering, curling and primping should be as enjoyable as possible. They can be if you're surrounded with pretty fabrications.

## t and boudoir

From a female perspective, the hours spent in the bathroom washing, waxing, shaving, styling, plucking, powdering, curling and primping should be as enjoyable as possible. They *can* be if you surround yourself with pretty fabrications.

Finding a really nice shower curtain is next to impossible. Forget the price tags ... and the fair to middling fabric quality ... most of the retail offerings are limited in style and color. Here's your chance to sew a curtain — from a fabulous fabric — that adds real panache to your bath. Two of these curtain styles feature easy-to-master vertical and horizontal piecing techniques, and the third, made from ribbons, offers lots of design options in your chosen colors.

## piecing techniques

The standard built-in tub/shower requires a 72" x 72" curtain, however, most home décor fabric is only 54" to 60" wide. The extra inches come from piecing, a technique used in many home décor projects, such as curtains.

For a shower curtain, the *traditional piecing method* involves cutting two full-fabric-width panels in the required cutting length along the fabric's straight grain (i.e. parallel to the selvage). Then, to create the curtain width, one full-width panel is cut into partial-width panels that are joined to the selvage edges of the intact full-width panel. This joining process creates *vertical seams* at the edges of a center panel. The fabric's straight grain also runs vertically down the project length.

You can also use the fabric's width for the project's partial length (a technique called *railroading*) and piece a second railroaded panel at the first panel's lower edge in a *horizontal seam*. With railroading, the fabric's straight grain runs horizontally across the width of the project and the piecing of a partial width panel (to achieve the required cut length) is done in a horizontal seam. Both piecing methods are shown at right.

Piecing may also involve *matching* if your fabric is striped (like one of the featured curtains) or has a repeating pattern. The goal of matching is to achieve a "seamless" flow of the stripe or print in the project. With a stripe, directional print or fabric with a nap, the obvious piecing strategy is the traditional one with vertical seams. Railroading is an option if using a solid fabric without a nap or a non-directional print.

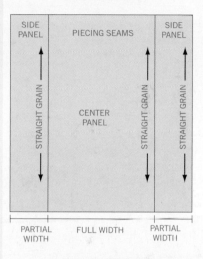

TRADITIONAL PIECING / STRAIGHT GRAIN RUNNING VERTICALLY

SIDE PANEL — PIECING SEAMS — SIDE PANEL

STRAIGHT GRAIN — CENTER PANEL — STRAIGHT GRAIN — STRAIGHT GRAIN

PARTIAL WIDTH — FULL WIDTH — PARTIAL WIDTH

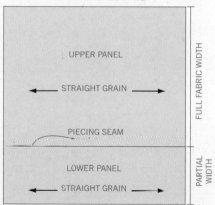

RAILROAD PIECING / STRAIGHT GRAIN RUNNING HORIZONTALLY

UPPER PANEL

STRAIGHT GRAIN

PIECING SEAM

LOWER PANEL

STRAIGHT GRAIN

FULL FABRIC WIDTH

PARTIAL WIDTH

# striped shower curtain

Stripes add vertical, orderly interest to any room, and with careful matching at the side seams, they proceed across this curtain without missing a step. The pinky peach and cream hues of this curtain walk on the soft side of regimental for boudoir appeal.

## materials

- ★ 4½ yd. 54"-wide striped decorator fabric for a 72" x 72" curtain (*Note*: Add extra yardage to make a longer curtain.)
- ★ Fusible seam tape
- ★ 12 large eyelets (¼" or wider) and eyelet-setting tools (*Note*: Make sure the eyelets you select are large enough to accommodate your shower curtain hooks or rings.)
- ★ Shower curtain liner

## instructions

**1** Measure and cut two 80"-long fabric panels, cutting their length down the straight grain and their width across the full fabric width, perpendicular to the selvage. The 80" length allows for a 1"-deep doubled header and a 3"-deep doubled hem, or a total of 8" for header and hem allowances. For a longer curtain, add 8" to the desired finished length and cut two panels in this length.

**2** To piece the panels, first trim the selvages from the panel edges. Press under a ½" seam allowance on the right edge of one panel (*side panel*). Apply fusible seam tape to the seam allowance.

**3** Place the second panel (*center panel*) right side up on a flat surface. Lap the side panel folded edge over the center panel left edge, keeping the panel upper and lower edges aligned, and adjust the overlapped edges so that the stripes match. Fuse the seam, then edgestitch close to the seam fold.

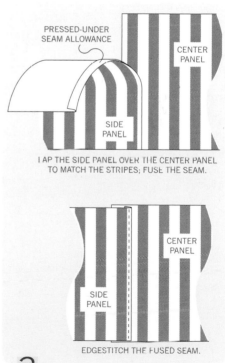

PRESSED-UNDER SEAM ALLOWANCE

CENTER PANEL

SIDE PANEL

LAP THE SIDE PANEL OVER THE CENTER PANEL TO MATCH THE STRIPES; FUSE THE SEAM.

CENTER PANEL

SIDE PANEL

EDGESTITCH THE FUSED SEAM.

3

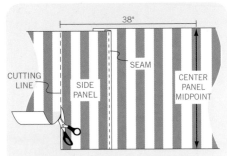

MEASURE 38" FROM THE CENTER PANEL MIDPOINT INTO THE SIDE PANEL. MARK A VERTICAL CUTTING LINE AND TRIM THE EXCESS SIDE PANEL.

4

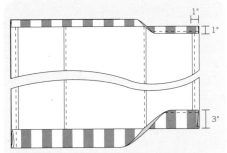

FINISH THE SIDE AND UPPER EDGES WITH 1"-DEEP DOUBLED HEMS. FINISH THE LOWER EDGE WITH A 3"-DEEP DOUBLED HEM.

6

**4** Measure 38" from the midpoint of the center panel and into the side panel, and mark a vertical line. Trim the excess side panel on the marked line.

**5** Repeat Steps 2, 3 and 4, using the remaining side panel fabric to piece a second panel to the center panel right edge, and trim the excess side panel. Follow the Finishing Seams instructions on page 177 to clean-finish the joining seam edges.

**6** To hem each side edge of the curtain, press under 1" twice and topstitch close to the inner fold. Repeat to topstitch a doubled 1"-deep header and a doubled 3"-deep hem.

**7** Align the shower curtain header with the liner upper edge and use the liner holes to mark 12 eyelet placements across the header. Follow the eyelet manufacturer's instructions to set an eyelet at each mark.

## curtain ring scrunchies

Hair scrunchies were the inspiration for these little ruffled collars that encircle the motifs of the shower curtain rings. You will need 2¾ yards of ⅞"-wide grosgrain ribbon or ½"-wide print ribbon for each scrunchie style. To prepare your ribbon, cut it into 12 lengths, 8" each. Fold under and glue ¼" on each cut edge.

For the checked ribbon scrunchie, wind elastic thread in your machine bobbin and use matching sewing thread in the machine needle. Leaving long thread tails at each end, stitch along one edge of the ribbon length. The elastic bobbin thread will automatically gather the ribbon and provide some stretch, too. Knot the thread tails so that the ribbon ends butt together. Twist/loop an elastic-edged scrunchie around each ring motif.

For the solid-color ribbon scrunchie, baste a line of gathering stitches along one ribbon edge. Follow the Gathering instructions on page 176 to pull threads and tightly gather the ribbon. Knot the threads at each end to secure the gathers and trim the excess thread. Wind a gathered scrunchie around each curtain ring motif.

# ruffled shower curtain

Blend Carmen Miranda with peach sherbet and add multiple rows of ruffles. That's the recipe for this peachy-keen shower curtain that Sarah says brings out her inner "mambo." The construction involves *railroading* or using the fabric's width as the project's partial length and then piecing the flounce-filled lower panel in a horizontal French seam.

## materials

- 5¼ yd. 54"-wide solid decorator fabric (*Note*: This yardage is sufficient to make a 72" x 72" curtain with four rows of ruffles. Because the fabric wrong side will show in the ruffles, select a woven fabric that looks nice on its right and wrong sides. Also, remember to purchase extra yardage to make a longer curtain.)

- Fusible seam tape

- 12 large eyelets (¼" or wider) and eyelet-setting tools (*Note*: Make sure the eyelets you select are large enough to accommodate your shower curtain hooks or rings.)

- Shower curtain liner

## sew the panels together

**1** Measure and cut two 76"-long fabric panels, cutting straight across the fabric width, perpendicular to the selvage. Trim the selvages from the panel edges.

**2** Fold one panel in half, widthwise, and cut it into two half-width panels, each measuring 27" x 76". One half-width panel will be used as the *lower panel* and will be pieced to the full-width *upper panel* to create the required curtain length. The second half-width panel, along with the remaining yardage, will be used to make the ruffles.

**3** Join the lower panel to the upper panel at their long edges in a horizontal French seam, following the French Seam instructions on page 177. Press the seam toward the lower panel.

**4** Position the assembled panels so that the seam runs horizontally across the lower portion of the curtain, then finish the sides, header and hem as shown in the Striped Shower Curtain Step 6 illustration on page 58.

## make and add the ruffles

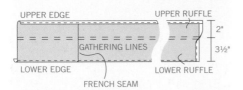

FOLD OVER ¼" ON RUFFLE UPPER EDGE TO THE RIGHT SIDE AND EDGESTITCH. FOLD UNDER ¼" ON THE LOWER EDGE AND EDGESTITCH. AT EACH END FOLD OVER ¼" TWICE TO THE RIGHT SIDE AND EDGESTITCH. BASTE TWO PARALLEL GATHERING LINES 2" FROM THE UPPER EDGE.

## 2

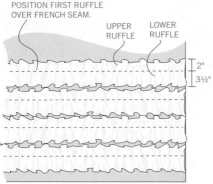

FUSE THE RUFFLES TO THE SEAM TAPE, THEN STITCH THE RUFFLES TO THE LOWER PANEL AS SHOWN.

## 5

**1** Cut 6"-wide strips (along the fabric length) from the remaining partial panel and yardage. Piece the strips, end-to-end, in French seams to create four lengths that are each approximately 144" (4 yards) long. *Note:* Do not worry if your strip lengths are a bit longer or shorter than 144", just make sure that all lengths are equal.

**2** To hem each strip and prepare it for gathering, *fold over* ¼" on the strip upper edge to the right side and edgestitch. *Fold under* ¼" on the strip lower edge to the wrong side and edgestitch. At the strip ends, fold over ¼" twice to the right side and edgestitch. Baste two parallel gathering lines 2" from the upper edge. These gathering lines create a 2"-deep upper ruffle and a 3½"-deep lower ruffle.

**3** Refer to the Gathering instructions on page 176 to pull threads and gather each strip to create a 72"-long ruffle.

**4** Adhere four evenly-spaced parallel lines of fusible seam tape, 5" apart, across the right side of the curtain lower panel, positioning the first tape line over the French seam.

**5** Position each ruffle, right-side up, over a line of fusible seam tape, making sure the gathered area of the ruffle is centered on the tape. Fuse the ruffles to the curtain lower panel. Now, sew each ruffle to the lower panel, stitching between the gathering lines. Remove the gathering stitches.

**6** Fold each upper ruffle over its lower ruffle on the stitched line and lightly press.

**7** Align the shower curtain header with the liner upper edge and use the liner holes to mark 12 eyelet placements across the header. Follow the eyelet manufacturer's instructions to set an eyelet at each mark.

# ribbon shower curtain

Emily loves the ribbon curtain concept, and intends to make one using lengths of ribbons and (knowing her) other cool arty materials. That's the beauty of this project. *You* become the "fabric" designer by choosing and arranging the ribbons as desired when you sew them into the header. The finished curtain will be 72" wide, but an inch or so longer than the standard 72" (helpful if you need a little extra length). If not, trim the ribbon ends.

## materials

- ★ ½ yd. 45"-wide cotton fabric for the curtain header in a solid or print that coordinates with your chosen ribbons
- ★ 1" x 74" strip of tear-away stabilizer (piece the strip if necessary)
- ★ Grosgrain ribbons, in your choice of colors, patterns and widths, in sufficient yardage so that when cut into 2-yd. lengths and placed edge-to-edge they measure 72". *Example*: You will need 162 yards of ⅞"-wide ribbons, or 84 yards of 1⅝"-wide ribbons.
- ★ Fusible seam tape
- ★ 12 large (¼" or wider) eyelets and eyelet-setting tools (*Note*: Make sure the eyelets you select are large enough to accommodate your shower curtain hooks or rings.)
- ★ Fray Check seam sealant
- ★ Shower curtain liner

## cutting instructions

From the curtain header fabric, cut:
- Two 8" x 37" panels (across the fabric width)

From the ribbons, cut:
- 2-yard lengths

## instructions

**1** Stack the ribbon lengths in order by color, style or randomly to create your "pattern."

**2** Stitch the curtain header panel short ends together; press the seam open. Press under ½" on each long edge of the header.

**3** Fold the header in half widthwise and stitch the short ends. Trim the seams, turn the header right-side out, and press the ends and header upper edge fold.

**4** Place one end of the tear-away stabilizer strip under your machine's presser foot and stitch about ½" down the strip center. Place the first ribbon length on the strip and stitch across its width to within ¼" of its opposite edge. With the needle down, lift the presser foot and butt the edge of the second ribbon length to the first. Lower the presser foot and stitch across the width of the second ribbon. Repeat to stitch all ribbon lengths to the stabilizer.

**5** Open the header lower edges and apply fusible seam tape over the lower layer seam allowance. Insert the stitched ribbons between the fabric layers, butting the side edge of the first ribbon to the header side seam. Fuse the ribbons to the header bottom layer. Fold the header upper layer over the ribbons. With the header layers aligned at their lower edges, edgestitch the header closed. Remove any tear-away stabilizer, as necessary.

**6** Align the shower curtain header with the liner upper edge and use the liner holes to mark 12 eyelet placements across the header upper edge. Follow the eyelet manufacturer's instructions to set an eyelet at each mark.

**7** Hang the curtain and liner, and trim the ribbon ends to the desired length. Apply Fray Check to the ribbon cut ends to prevent them from raveling.

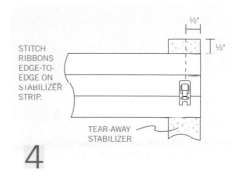

STITCH RIBBONS EDGE-TO-EDGE ON STABILIZER STRIP.

TEAR-AWAY STABILIZER

**4**

FUSE RIBBONS TO HEADER BOTTOM LAYER.

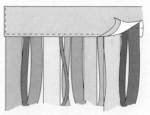

FOLD HEADER UPPER LAYER OVER RIBBONS AND EDGESTITCH.

**5**

## beribboned towels

Ribbons make dandy trims for hand towels. The brown towel sports a cocoa-colored ribbon and copper-toned buttons; the blue wears matching layers of grosgrain and soft chenille rickrack; and the coral has a perky polka dot trim. Sew simple! Apply fusible seam tape to the towel's woven border and fuse your chosen ribbon in place, turning under ½" of excess ribbon at the towel edges and securing with fabric glue. Use your machine to edgestitch the ribbons, and to attach buttons, another layer of trim or other adornments.

In its original state, this garage sale screen had cardboard panels set into its unfinished wood frames. Wallpaper was probably intended to cover the panels, but as fabric is my medium, I removed the cardboard and installed quilted panels instead.

Each panel is essentially a quilt "sandwich" consisting of three layers: the striped fabric, low-loft quilt batting, and a coordinating quilt-weight back fabric. All layers were cut 2" wider and longer than the frame openings, and then pinned together, marked with crisscrossing diagonal stitching lines, and machine-quilted by stitching through all layers on the marked lines.

To insert each panel in its frame, I squeezed fabric glue in the center of the frame upper edge crevice, folded about 1" of the quilted panel upper edge over the blade of a dull knife and pushed it into the glue-filled opening. After gluing the panel upper edge, I repeated this process to glue the lower edge, and then moved on the side edges, making sure the fabric panel was taut top-to-bottom and side-to-side as I glued.

To make a similar screen, look for one with a groove or crevice in the frame that will allow you to insert/glue the quilted panel edges. A fireplace screen or an old window frame (without the glass) may work nicely for this project, too. Even an old screen door can become the new quilted closure for a powder room or linen closet.

dressing room screen

## linen jewelry bag

Dave recently asked me how many vintage napkins I've purchased at house sales, and did I really think I should buy more when I hardly ever use them? "It's not the *using* that's important, dear, it's the *having*," I replied patiently. For this drawstring bag, I sacrificed two of my precious pink cocktail napkins with fleurs-de-lis embroidery. This sew-easy bag can be sized up with a dinner-size napkin or yardage instead of napkins to hold larger items, such as shoes, lingerie or a special gift.

## materials

★ 2 rectangular linen cocktail napkins or 1 square linen napkin (*Note*: The featured project was made with two 5½" x 8¾" cocktail napkins.)

★ 1½ yd. of ⅜"-wide coordinating ribbon

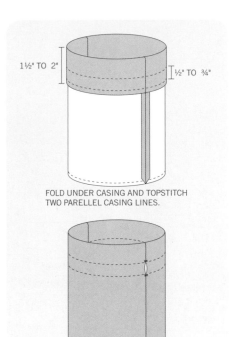

1½" TO 2"    ½" TO ¾"

FOLD UNDER CASING AND TOPSTITCH
TWO PARELLEL CASING LINES.

TURN BAG AND CLIP SEAM STITCHES
WITHIN CASING LINES. TACK SEAM
ABOVE AND BELOW EACH OPENING.

2

## to make a bag using two cocktail napkins

**1** Pin the napkins together. Stitch around three edges, pivoting at corners, using a ¼" seam allowance. Leave one shorter edge open. Press the longer side seams open at their upper open edges, and turn the bag right-side out.

**2** To make the drawstring casing, fold under 1½"-2" on the open edge and press. Stitch two parallel casing lines around the open edge as shown. Clip the seams between the casing stitches to create openings for the ribbons; tack the upper and lower edges of each casing opening.

**3** Cut the ribbon into two equal lengths. Use a safety pin or bodkin to thread one length through the casing, beginning and ending at the same opening. Repeat to thread the second ribbon length through the opposite casing opening.

**4** Adjust the ribbon tails so that they are equal in length, trimming extra length if desired. Tie each pair of tails in an overhand knot. Pull at the ribbon knots to close the bag.

## to make a bag using one napkin

**1** Fold the napkin in half and press. Stitch around three edges (including the folded edge), pivoting at corners and leaving one shorter edge open. Clip the folded edge to open the seam. Press the side seams open, and then turn the bag right-side out.

**2** Follow Steps 2, 3 and 4 above to finish the bag.

THE SHELF BACK REVEALS ITS U SHAPE AND PREMADE SCREW HOLES FOR MOUNTING.

Peggy owns Sew Creative, a local fabric store (see the Resources on page 188), and kindly offered to machine embroider "make me *blush*" on the skirt fabric for this little shelf. After this embroidery was complete, it took me just 30 minutes to stitch the skirt, staple its upper edge to a small, flat-edged shelf, and finish the upper and side edges with gimp braid.

*make me blush shelf*

## materials

* ★ 10"-wide x 3¾"-deep U-shaped shelf
* ★ ⅓ yd. 45"- or 54"-wide fabric
* ★ 1 yd. matching gimp or other desired trim
* ★ Staple gun and ¼" or ⅜" staples
* ★ Fabric glue

## instructions

**1** Cut a 27"-wide x 10"-long strip of fabric for the featured shelf. If your shelf is longer and/or deeper, measure its outward perimeter, add 6" for the corner pleats and 1" for the seam allowances, and use this measurement for the strip cutting width.

**2** If you desire message(s) or motif(s) embroidered on your skirt, consult a local embroidery service (sewing machine dealerships are a great source) and explain your project. Be sure to bring your shelf and fabric to review the skirt construction with your embroiderer. Ideally, the embroidery stitching should be centered both in the skirt length and width along the shelf front.

**3** Fold the skirt panel in half lengthwise to measure 5" x 27"; stitch the short side edges. Trim the seams, turn the panel right-side out, and press the seams and lower edge fold. Baste the upper raw edges together.

**4** Pin-mark the center of the skirt upper raw edge. Mark the center of the shelf front edge. Align the skirt and shelf center marks and staple the skirt to the shelf within the skirt upper edge seam allowance.

**5** Working from the skirt/shelf center and outward left and right, staple the skirt upper edge to the shelf front edge. At the corners, create 1½"-deep half-pleats and staple them to the shelf edge. Continue stapling the skirt to the shelf sides, ending at its back edges.

**6** Finish the skirt by gluing gimp or other trim over the upper raw edges and, if desired, down the skirt length that butts the wall.

**7** Mount the shelf following the manufacturer's instructions.

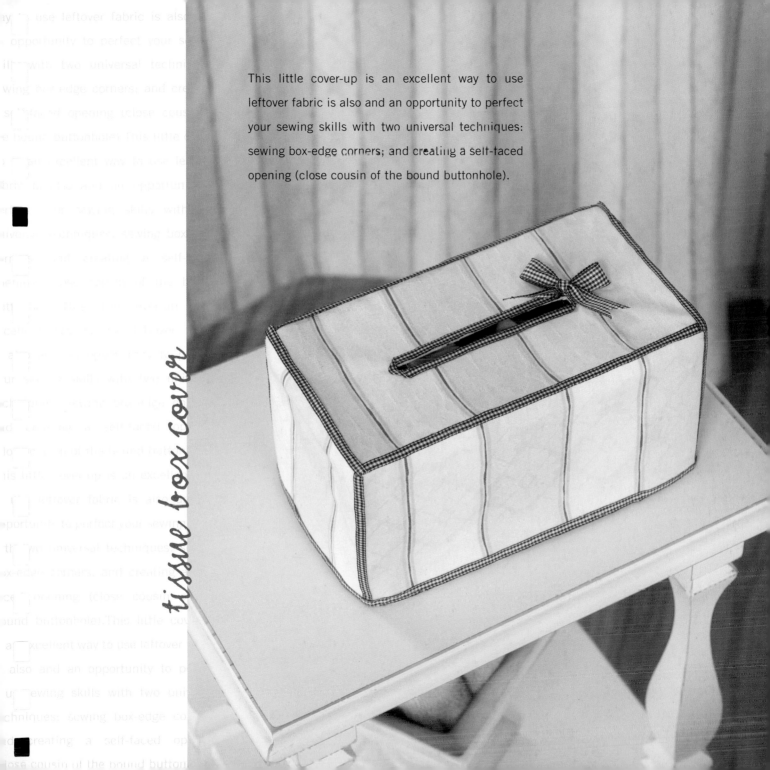

This little cover-up is an excellent way to use leftover fabric is also and an opportunity to perfect your sewing skills with two universal techniques: sewing box-edge corners; and creating a self-faced opening (close cousin of the bound buttonhole).

tissue box cover

## materials

- ★ ¼ yd. cotton fabric
- ★ ¼ yd. heavy-weight fusible interfacing
- ★ 2 yd. ¼"-wide coordinating ribbon to trim the seams, hem and tissue opening (optional)
- ★ ½ yd. ⅜"-wide coordinating ribbon for the bow (optional)
- ★ Fabric glue

*instructions*

1   Fuse the heavy-weight interfacing to the fabric wrong side following the manufacturer's instructions.

2   Measure the top and each side of the tissue box you would like to cover. Add 1" to each dimension. Cut the five corresponding panels from the interfaced fabric.

3   Pin the four side panels together in the proper order to fit around the box. Stitch the side seams, leaving ½" unstitched at the panel upper edges; press the seams open. Press under and topstitch a ½"-deep hem around the panel lower edges.

4   To make the tissue opening in the top panel, first determine the desired length of this opening. From the interfaced fabric, cut a 3"-wide facing that is 3" longer that the opening's determined length. *Note:* The sample project features a 6"-long opening. Thus, the cutting dimensions of its facing are 3" x 9". Press under and topstitch a ¼"-deep hem on each facing edge.

5   To attach the facing, mark the stitching and slit lines on the facing wrong side as shown. Pin the facing to the top panel, centering it exactly between the side and upper and lower edges. Stitch the facing to the top panel on the marked stitching lines.

6   Starting from the center and working outward, slit the opening on the marked lines using small sharp scissors; be careful not to cut into the machine stitches as you make the diagonal slits at the corners. Turn the facing to the top panel wrong side so that the facing seams form the edges of the opening. Press well. Edgestitch the opening.

7   Refer to the Box-Edge Corners instructions beginning on page 178 to assemble the side and top panels.

8   If desired, glue ¼"-wide ribbon trim over the seams, around the lower edge hem, and around the tissue opening edges. Use ⅜"-wide ribbon to form a bow and glue it to one corner of the opening.

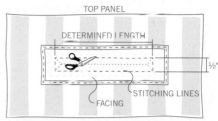

CENTER FACING ON TOP PANEL. STITCH FACING TO PANEL ON MARKED STITCHING LINES. SLIT OPENING ON MARKED SLIT LINES THROUGH ALL LAYERS.

5

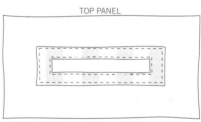

TURN FACING TO TOP PANEL WRONG SIDE AND PRESS FLAT. EDGESTITCH THE OPENING.

6

vanity stool cushions

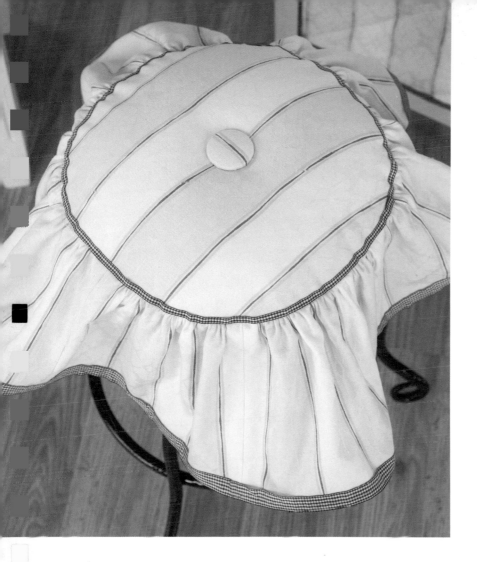

A stool is no fool—it says "Cushion me!" Slip on the basic round model, or make one with a sassy skirt. If your stool seat diameter is greater than 12", just add 1" to its diameter to cut the fabric circles. Resize the band panels to fit by measuring the stool seat circumference and adding 1" for seam allowances.

## materials

- ★ 54"-wide decorator fabric:
  - ½ yd. for the basic 12"-diameter cushion
  - 1 yd. for the 12"-diameter cushion with skirt
- ★ 1½ yd. ⅜"-wide elastic
- ★ 12"-diameter round pillow form or polyester fiberfill
- ★ Decorative ribbon (optional)
- ★ 1⅝"-diameter cover button (optional)

## make the basic 12"-diameter cushion

**1** Cut two 13"-diameter circles and one 41"-long x 5"-deep band strip from the fabric. *Note:* Cut the band strip across the fabric width.

**2** Stitch the band strip short ends to create a circular band; press the seam open. Fold the band in half, wrong sides together, to measure 2½" deep; press the folded edge. Baste the band raw edges using a ⅜" seam allowance. Topstitch ⅝" from the band folded edge to create a casing for the elastic.

**3** Follow the Joining Curved and Straight Edges instructions on page 183 to baste the band raw edge around the edge of one fabric circle, using a ⅜" seam allowance.

**4** With the band sandwiched in between, stitch the second circle to the first circle/band edges in a ½" seam, leaving approximately 10" unstitched for turning. Trim and notch the seam allowance. Turn the cushion right-side out and press.

**5** Insert the pillow form or the desired amount of fiberfill into the cushion cover. Fold under the seam allowances on the cushion open edges and whipstitch them closed.

**6** Use your seam ripper to carefully cut several machine stitches at the band seam within the casing to allow for elastic insertion. Attach a bodkin or safety pin to one end of the elastic and thread it through the casing, beginning and ending at the clipped seam opening.

**7** Overlap and pin the elastic ends. Adjust the band gathers evenly. Place the band over your stool to test its fit and increase the elastic overlap if necessary.

**8** Stitch the elastic together with three or four tight zigzag rows and trim the excess. Tuck the stitched elastic ends inside the casing and whipstitch the casing closed. Finished, the cushion underside should resemble the upper left photo.

## optional embellishments

For either cushion, if desired, cover a purchased cover button according to the manufacturer's instructions, and sew the button to the cushion right side center, through all layers, to create a tuft. Also, if desired, use fabric glue to adhere decorative ribbon around the cushion edge and/or the skirt hem.

## make the skirted cushion

**1** Follow Step 1 on the previous page to cut the circles and band strip. Also cut two 8"-deep panels across the fabric width for the gathered skirt.

**2** To make the skirt, piece the panel short ends to create a circular band measuring between 62" (for 1½ times fullness) to 82" (for double fullness); press the piecing seams open. Press under and topstitch a doubled ¼"-deep hem on the skirt lower edge. Refer to the Gathering instructions on page 176 to gather the skirt upper raw edge to measure 41".

**3** Pin the skirt gathered edge around one fabric circle. Adjust the gathers evenly, then baste the skirt to the circle using a ⅜" seam allowance.

**4** Follow Step 2 on the previous page to make the band strip and topstitch the elastic casing.

**5** Keeping the gathered skirt turned toward the first circle center, follow Step 3 on the previous page to baste the band raw edge around the fabric circle edge.

**6** Now, keeping both the band and skirt folded toward the center of the first circle, follow Step 4 on the previous page to stitch the second and first circles together, leaving an opening for turning.

**7** Follow Step 5 on the previous page to turn the cushion, stuff it with a pillow form or fiberfill, and whipstitch the cushion edges closed. Follow Steps 6, 7 and 8 to insert elastic into the casing and finish the cushion so that its underside resembles the photo at right.

WITH SKIRT OR WITHOUT, THE ELASTIC-EDGED BAND ON EACH CUSHION CREATES A CUSTOM FIT.

# bedroom in transition

# in transition

Start with a twin-size bed, add a quilted Matelassé coverlet in white, and paint the walls a deep ruby red. These are the constant elements in this mix-and-match collection of projects that transition the room from a girl's tented hideaway to a young lady's boudoir and, later, to masculine guest quarters.

*matelassé coverlet with zigzag band*

What goes on your bed? The best cover, in my opinion, is a quilted coverlet, and the best material for a quilted coverlet is Matelassé, a fabric with interesting surface texture that resembles quilting. Add batting, lining and machine quilting, and Matelassé makes a spectacular bed!

## materials

* 54"- to 60"-wide Matelassé or similarly textured fabric in the determined yardage
* Low-loft quilt batting in coverlet size
* Muslin for coverlet backing in the determined yardage
* Round saucer or plate for tracing

## determine dimensions and yardages

**1** Measure the width, length and depth of your mattress to determine the desired overall *finished width and length* of your coverlet. Enter these dimensions in the blank spaces above the chart. *Note:* Use this opportunity to make a generously sized coverlet by adding extra inches to its width and length.

**2** Using these determined dimensions, refer to the chart below to calculate the cutting dimensions of a center panel (cut across the full width of your chosen fabric) and the band panel with corner pleats.

Center Panel and Band Panel Cutting Dimensions for a Coverlet with an Overall Finished Width of _____" and Finished Length of _____"

| | |
|---|---|
| center panel cut width | fabric width with selvages removed |
| center panel cut length | (finished length + 5½") - band cut depth |
| band cut depth | (finished width - center panel cut width) ÷ 2 + 2" |
| band cut length* | finished width + (finished length x 2) + 10" |

*Note:* Cut and piece the band panels end-to-end to achieve the required length.

**3** Using the cutting dimensions determined above, follow the instructions for Drawing a Sample Cutting Layout on page 187 to create a layout and determine the required yardage of both the Matelassé and muslin fabrics.

### Tip

Even 60"-wide Matelassé fabric is a bit skimpy for a twin-size coverlet, thus piecing some extra fabric is necessary. For this project, the extra inches come from the zigzag-edged bands around the coverlet side and lower edges.

matelassé coverlet with zigzag band matelass

## assemble the coverlet

1 Cut the center panel (trimming off the selvages), one batting panel, and one muslin panel; piece the muslin backing panel as necessary using the determined center panel dimensions as your guide.

2 On a flat surface, layer the muslin backing, wrong-side up, the batting, and the center panel, right-side up, and pin the layers. Follow the Matelassé woven pattern or measure and mark the desired quilting lines, and machine-quilt this panel on the marked lines.

3 Fold under and topstitch a doubled 1½"-deep hem at the panel upper edge.

4 Trace around a saucer or plate at the panel lower edge corners, and cut on the traced lines to curve them.

5 Cut and piece the Matelassé band panel and a muslin lining panel in the determined band panel cutting dimensions. Pin the band and lining panels together and stitch their short ends. To create the zigzag edge, stitch along the band lower edge following the fabric's woven pattern. If the fabric doesn't have woven markings, draw the desired edge motif on the band fabric and stitch on the marked lines.

6 Trim the excess band and lining at the band lower edge, clipping corners and curves as necessary. Turn the band right-side out and press flat.

7 Pin-fit the band around the center panel side and lower edges, forming 4"-wide inverted pleats at the panel curved corners. Remove the band and baste across the pleat upper edges.

8 Follow the Attaching Bands instructions on page 173 to stitch the band around the center panel edges and slipstitch the lining in place.

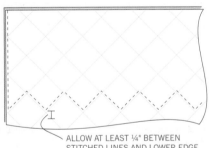

ALLOW AT LEAST ¼" BETWEEN STITCHED LINES AND LOWER EDGE.

STITCH BAND AND LINING PANELS AT SIDE AND LOWER EDGES. TO CREATE ZIGZAG EDGE, STITCH ALONG FABRIC'S WOVEN PATTERN OR MARKED LINES.

5

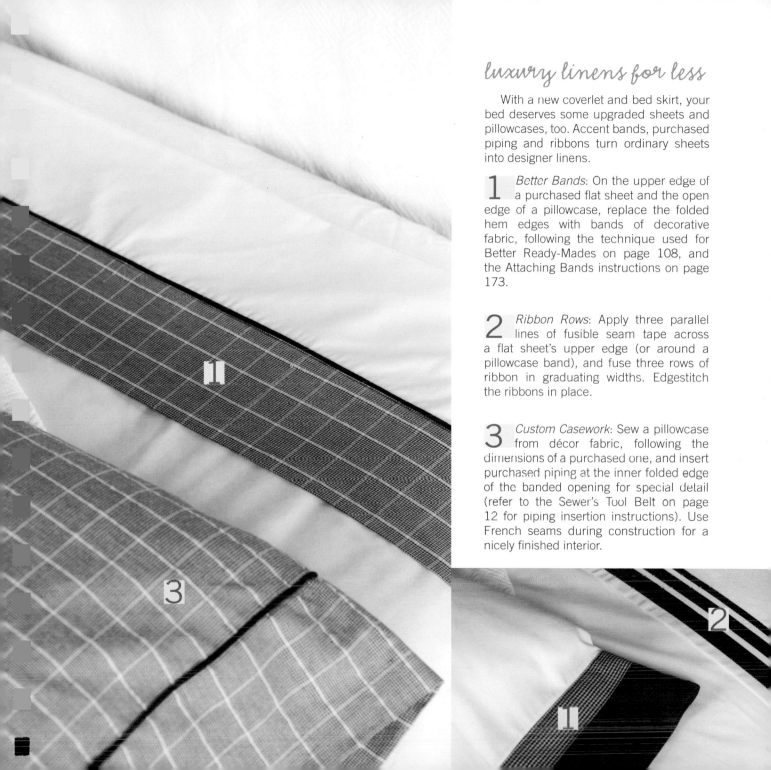

## luxury linens for less

With a new coverlet and bed skirt, your bed deserves some upgraded sheets and pillowcases, too. Accent bands, purchased piping and ribbons turn ordinary sheets into designer linens.

**1** *Better Bands*: On the upper edge of a purchased flat sheet and the open edge of a pillowcase, replace the folded hem edges with bands of decorative fabric, following the technique used for Better Ready-Mades on page 108, and the Attaching Bands instructions on page 173.

**2** *Ribbon Rows*: Apply three parallel lines of fusible seam tape across a flat sheet's upper edge (or around a pillowcase band), and fuse three rows of ribbon in graduating widths. Edgestitch the ribbons in place.

**3** *Custom Casework*: Sew a pillowcase from décor fabric, following the dimensions of a purchased one, and insert purchased piping at the inner folded edge of the banded opening for special detail (refer to the Sewer's Tool Belt on page 12 for piping insertion instructions). Use French seams during construction for a nicely finished interior.

## T-shirt memory quilt

Once your child joins the band, an athletic team or service group, the T-shirt collection begins. You can turn this collection into a memory quilt that incorporates leftover fabrics from other projects or one made entirely from Ts. Follow these guidelines:

- Decide on a quilt theme and select shirts accordingly. (The featured quilt includes conference, sectional and state swim meet competitions, as well as life guard shirts, all worn during senior year in high school.)
- Use T-shirts that are in good condition (no stains, rips, etc. in the printed areas).
- Consider color coordination. For example, use blue and red shirts only, and reject the neon green and orange ones (or vice versa).
- The back of the shirt may contain a message that's as important as the front one. You can cut, fuse and satin stitch a back message/ motif onto the cutout front ... a two-for-one block design!
- To stabilize the stretchy cotton knit fabric and make it easier to join to other blocks, fuse lightweight interfacing to the shirt wrong side, covering the area you intend to use before cutting the block.

The featured quilt measures 47" x 62" and consists of six T-shirt blocks and six fabric blocks. To make a similar quilt, follow these general instructions:

**1** Select shirts from which to cut 16" x 16" interfaced blocks. Apply lightweight fusible web to the wrong side of any motif you intend to use as an appliqué and cut it out. Fuse the appliqué to the block right side, positioning it as desired, and satin stitch its edges. Repeat to cut a total of six 16" x 16" T-shirt blocks.

**2** Cut two 16" x 16" blocks each from three coordinating print or solid cotton fabrics.

**3** To assemble the quilt top, arrange the T-shirt and fabric blocks in four horizontal rows of three blocks each, arranging the blocks as desired. Stitch the blocks in horizontal rows, with ½" seams, end-to-end, and press all seams open. Stitch the horizontal rows at the upper/lower edges to finish assembling the quilt top.

**4** Cut a 52" x 67" panel from a coordinating fabric for the quilt back. Place it wrong-side up on a flat surface and layer low-loft quilt batting on top. Center the quilt top, right-side up, on top of these layers. Pin the layers and machine quilt them by stitching directly over the seams using straight or decorative stitches, as desired.

**5** Baste around the quilt top, ½" from its edges. Fold the excess backing fabric to the quilt front in doubled hems approximately 1" deep. Position the hem inner folds to slightly overlap the basting stitches, and topstitch the hems.

THIS COLORFUL QUILT COMBINES SIX LARGE T-SHIRT BLOCKS WITH A MIX OF DÉCOR PRINTS.

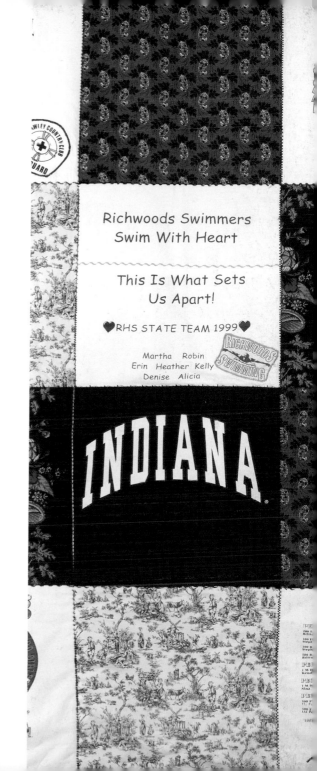

quick-change layered bed skirts

FULL-LENGTH FLAT PANEL SKIRT.

GATHERED SKIRT.

A coverlet needs a bed skirt, but the conventional skirt has problems. It shifts and sags when you tuck in sheets and blankets under the mattress. Ellen *hates* when this happens and asks, "Isn't there a better way to make a bed skirt?" Yes! You can have your skirt, make it stay put, remove for it cleaning, add another layer to it, and switch it for another skirt ... all without tugging, tucking or removing the mattress. How? With Velcro!

## materials

* Mattress pad with sides and elastic edges that fit your box spring snugly
* Bed skirt fabric in the determined yardage
* Sew-in Velcro tape (both hook and loop sections) in the determined yardages
* Skirt lining fabric in the determined yardage (flat panel style only)
* Packaged double-fold bias binding tape (available in the notions section of any fabric store)
* Fabric glue

## attach the Velcro to the mattress pad

1   To determine the Velcro tape yardage, measure and add together the two side lengths and lower edge length of your box springs. Divide this figure by 36". You will need this yardage of both Velcro hook and Velcro loop tape for one skirt. If you intend to layer a second bed skirt, purchase double this determined yardage.

2   Remove the mattress from the box spring and cover the box spring with the mattress pad. On the pad top, mark the location of the Velcro tape down each side and across the lower edge about 1" to 2" inside the box spring edges. Remove the pad and use the marked lines to position and edgestitch Velcro hook tape to the pad.

WITH VELCRO HOOK TAPE SEWN ON THE MATTRESS PAD 1" TO 2" INSIDE THE BOX SPRING, THE BED SKIRT'S UPPER EDGES SHOULD NEVER PEEK OUT.

## make the full-length flat panel skirt

**1** This skirt style features five separate panels: two side panels; one end panel; and two corner flap panels. See the diagram below to measure your bed, and refer to the following chart to determine the cutting dimensions for each panel. Follow the Creating a Sample Layout instructions on page 187 to calculate both the skirt fabric and lining yardages.

| | | |
|---|---|---|
| side panel cutting dimensions | (side panel width + 1") x (panel length + 1") | cut two each from the skirt and lining fabrics |
| lower panel cutting dimensions | (lower panel width + 1") x (panel length + 1") | cut one each from the skirt and lining fabrics |
| corner flap cutting dimensions | (corner flap width + 1") x (panel length + 1") | cut two each from the skirt and lining fabrics |

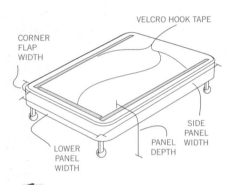

VELCRO HOOK TAPE

CORNER FLAP WIDTH

SIDE PANEL WIDTH

PANEL DEPTH

LOWER PANEL WIDTH

1

**2** Cut out the required skirt panels as indicated above. Stitch a lining panel to each fabric panel at the side and lower edges. *Note:* Follow the Step 7 and 8 instructions for the Matelassé Coverlet with Zigzag Band on page 82 to create a unique lower edge treatment, if desired.

**3** Turn each panel right-side out and press the seams flat. Baste the upper raw edges. Finish them with double-fold bias binding tape, following the tape manufacturer's instructions. *Note:* Attaching pre-made bias tape is similar to the bias binding technique; see Cutting and Applying Bias Binding on page 180.

**4** Edgestitch Velcro loop tape to the wrong-side upper edge of each skirt panel. Adhere the panel upper edges to the mattress pad/box spring hook tape to attach the skirt. *Note:* Fold and stitch tucks in the flap upper edges for a better fit around the box spring corners.

## make the gathered skirt

**1** Refer to the bed diagram on the previous page to measure and add together the box spring side and bottom lengths; multiply this figure by 1.5 or 2, depending on the desired skirt fullness. The resulting figure is the skirt cut length.

**2** Determine the skirt's finished depth by measuring from the box spring Velcro to the floor. Add 1" to this measurement for the skirt panel cut depth. *Note:* If layering this skirt over an underskirt, determine its desired shorter finished depth.

**3** Follow the Drawing a Sample Cutting Layout instructions on page 187 to create a sample layout and calculate the required skirt yardage.

**4** Cut and piece panels to create the required cut length. Finish the short edges, and then the lower edge with doubled ¼"-deep topstitched hems. Follow the Gathering instructions on page 176 to machine baste the skirt upper raw edge to fit around the box spring edges. Pin-fit the gathered skirt to the box spring and adjust the gathers evenly. Remove the skirt and stitch the skirt upper edge to secure the gathers.

**5** Finish the skirt upper edge with double-fold bias binding tape and Velcro loop tape, following Steps 3 and 4 on the previous page. *Note:* If using this skirt as a top layer, glue Velcro loop tape over the right-side upper edge of the full-length underskirt.

THE GATHERED SKIRT ADDS AN EXTRA LAYER OF PRETTY RUFFLES OVER A LONGER EYELET UNDERSKIRT.

THE SAME SKIRT CAN BE USED AS A SINGLE-LAYER TREATMENT, TOO.

bolster and flange pillows

A throw pillow and some bolsters make the bed, the latter coming in handy during sleepover pillow fights. Mixing and matching the fabrics on flanges and panels keeps the décor theme going, too.

# bolster cover

## materials

* 12" x 36" bolster pillow form
* 1¼ yd. 54"-wide decorator fabric for the sides
* ½ yd. 54"-wide decorator fabric for the ends
* Matching embroidery floss (optional)

## cutting instructions

From the side fabric, cut:
  * One 37" x 39" side panel

From the end fabric, cut:
  * Two 13"-diameter round end panels

## instructions

**1** Stitch the side panel 37"-long edges, leaving 12" unslitched in the center of the seam, to create a tube. Press the seam open. Follow the Joining Curved and Straight Edges instructions on page 183 to stitch a round panel to each tube end. Turn the cover right-side out and press.

**2** Insert the bolster pillow form through the opening. Fold under the seam allowances on the opening edges and whipstitch the opening closed.

**3** If desired, use embroidery thread to hand-stitch a running stitch around each end panel edge, about ½" from the seam. *Note:* This bit of hand stitching creates a mini flange and results in a snugger fit at the bolster ends.

# flange pillow

## materials

- ★ 18" x 18" pillow form
- ★ ⅔ yd. 54"-wide solid decorator fabric for the front and back
- ★ ¾ yd. 54"-wide print decorator fabric for the flange
- ★ 3 flat buttons, ¾" diameter
- ★ 2½ yd. ¼"-wide grosgrain ribbon

## cutting instructions

From the solid front and back fabric, cut:
- ★ One 19" x 19" back panel
- ★ Two 11" x 9" front panels

From the print flange fabric, cut:
- ★ Eight 28" x 4½" flange strips (Note: Cut the strips along the fabric lengthwise grain to conserve yardage.)

# instructions

**1** Hem the front panel 9"-long overlapping edges by pressing under ½" and then 2"; edgestitch close to each inner fold.

**2** On one front panel hemmed edge, mark three evenly-spaced vertical buttonholes, large enough to accommodate the selected buttons. Machine-stitch the buttonholes and cut them open.

**3** Overlap the front panels (with the buttonholed panel on top) so that their combined width equals 19". On the under panel, mark the button placements through the cut buttonholes. Use your machine to stitch a button at each mark.

**4** Button the panels, adjust the overlap to assure the 19" width measurement and baste across the upper and lower overlapped edges. Now, treat these overlapped panels as one panel.

**5** To assemble four strips each for the front and back flanges, arrange the strips as shown and fold the upper strip end diagonally at each corner. Press the upper strip folds and mark the corresponding foldlines on the lower strips.

**6** Pin the strips, matching the diagonal pressed foldlines with the diagonal marked lines, and stitch all flange corners. Trim the excess fabric and press the seams open.

**7** Pin then stitch the front panel edges to the inner edges of the square flange, referring to the Box-Edge Corners instructions on page 178. Repeat to assemble the back panel and the second square flange.

**8** Stitch the pillow front/flange to the pillow back/flange around the flange edges. Trim the seams and corners, turn the cover right side out through the button opening, and press the flange edges flat.

**9** Pin the front and back panel edges, wrong sides together, with their seams exactly aligned. Stitch over the seams to close the panel edges. If desired, glue lengths of ribbon over these stitched seams, and tie the ribbon ends in bows at the corners. Insert the pillow form through the button opening.

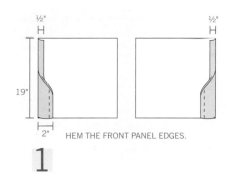

HEM THE FRONT PANEL EDGES.

**1**

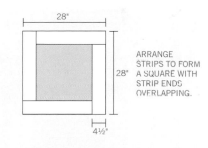

OVERLAP PANELS AND MARK BUTTON PLACEMENTS ON THE UNDER PANEL THROUGH THE CUT BUTTONHOLES.

**3**

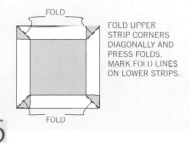

ARRANGE STRIPS TO FORM A SQUARE WITH STRIP ENDS OVERLAPPING.

FOLD UPPER STRIP CORNERS DIAGONALLY AND PRESS FOLDS. MARK FOLD LINES ON LOWER STRIPS.

**5**

Now that you've
dressed your bed,
it's time to drape
it with a canopy.

# tent canopy

You've seen them in stores and catalogs ... those gauzy renditions of old-fashioned mosquito netting. I was stumped about how to construct a similar canopy until Marilyn offered the answer to my engineering problem. She suggested using a quilting hoop. Eureka! This two-section canopy was born.

- ★ 24"-diameter round quilting hoop (*Note*: Look in the quilting section of a fabric store for paired balsa hoops with an outer hoop separating with a block-screwed closure and a solid inner hoop.)
- ★ 9½ yd. sheer or opaque curtain fabric, netting or gauze scrim for the canopy skirt and topper (*Note*: This yardage is sufficient for a canopy to hang from an 8-foot-high ceiling. Add 1½ yards for each additional foot of ceiling height.)
- ★ 1 yd. 45"-wide crisp cotton or organza fabric for the canopy collar
- ★ 8 yd. beaded trim
- ★ Large decorative tassel with hanging loop or tasseled curtain tieback
- ★ 12" of narrow cord, ribbon or sturdy string
- ★ Staple gun and ¾" staples
- ★ Cup hook suitable for mounting in a ceiling
- ★ Fabric glue
- ★ Wood glue

*instructions*

**1** To prepare the quilting hoops for their separate treatments, use a flat screwdriver head to carefully pry loose and remove the wood blocks from the outer hoop. Examine the inner hoop edge for a joint where the balsa layers have been joined. Carefully bend the hoop at this joint until it breaks apart. As an alternative, use a serrated knife to open the inner hoop with a diagonal cut. Set the hoops aside.

**2** To assemble the canopy skirt, cut three 8-foot-long panels of skirt/topper fabric, cutting each across the full width of the fabric. Stitch the panels together at the selvage edges in two French seams, following the French seam instructions on page 177; leave the remaining selvage edges open.

**3** Create a hoop casing at the skirt upper edge by topstitching a doubled 1½"-deep hem. Finish the skirt lower edge in a doubled ¾"-deep topstitched hem.

**4** Glue or edgestitch the bead trim over the skirt right side selvage edges; make sure to leave the hoop casing ends open if edgestitching the trim.

**5** With the skirt right side facing outward, thread the inner hoop through the skirt upper edge casing. Butt the hoop ends and glue them together with wood glue. Let the glue dry thoroughly, and then adjust the skirt gathers to cover this glued joint.

**6** To assemble the canopy topper, cut two 18"-deep panels across the fabric width from the remaining skirt yardage. Piece/trim the panels to measure 72" wide x 18" deep. Follow the Step 3 instructions above with these exceptions: Create a lower edge 1½"-deep hoop casing, and finish the upper edge in a doubled ¾"-deep topstitched hem.

**7** To make the topper lower edge collar, cut two 12"-deep panels across the width of the collar fabric. Stitch the panel short edges in a French seam. Trim the joined panels to measure 73" wide. Fold the collar in half to measure 6" x 73", and stitch the panel short ends.

**8** Mark the desired zigzag stitching line along the collar folded edge. Stitch on the marked lines, then trim the excess fabric and clip the interior corners. Turn right side out and press flat. Clean-finish the collar upper edge.

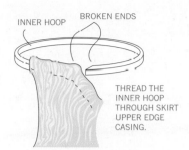

INNER HOOP  BROKEN ENDS

THREAD THE INNER HOOP THROUGH SKIRT UPPER EDGE CASING.

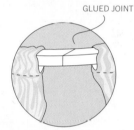

GLUED JOINT

BUTT AND GLUE THE INNER HOOP BROKEN ENDS. ADJUST CURTAIN GATHERS TO COVER GLUED JOINT.

**5**

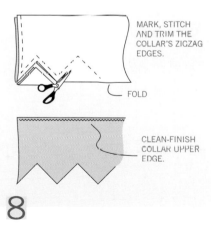

MARK, STITCH AND TRIM THE COLLAR'S ZIGZAG EDGES.

FOLD

CLEAN-FINISH COLLAR UPPER EDGE.

**8**

*canopies three bed canopies three bed canop*

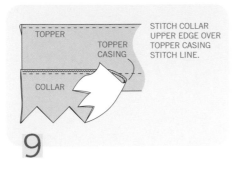

**TOPPER**

**TOPPER CASING**

STITCH COLLAR UPPER EDGE OVER TOPPER CASING STITCH LINE.

**COLLAR**

**9**

**9** Stitch the collar upper edge over the topper casing stitches as shown. Glue or edgestitch the beaded trim over the collar upper edge.

**10** To close the topper upper edge, use a small safety pin to thread the cord or string through the topstitched hem. Gather the edge tightly, knot the cord and trim the excess.

**11** With the topper/collar right side facing outward, thread the outer hoop through the topper casing. *Note:* Allow 1" to 1½" of topper casing to extend beyond one hoop end.

**12** Adjust the inner hoop curtain gathers evenly. Place the outer hoop over the inner hoop so that the outer hoop open edges are opposite the curtain open edges. Be careful not to align the inner hoop glued joint with the outer hoop open edges.

**13** Fold the organza collar up to reveal the topper casing. At one outer hoop end, press the hoops together as tightly as possible with one hand and use your other hand to staple the hoops together. Move several inches to the left or right, and repeat until the outer hoop has been completely stapled to the inner hoop. *Note:* The outer hoop won't fit exactly around the inner hoop because of the fabric bulk, thus the purpose of the 1" to 1½" casing extension created in Step 11 above. Overlap and glue this casing extension end over its beginning edge.

**14** Install the cup hook in the ceiling at the desired location. Insert the curtain tieback hook or tassel loop from inside the canopy through the small opening in the topper gathers and hang on the hook.

AS A HANGER, A TASSELED TIEBACK LIKE THIS ONE LOOKS NICE FROM THE OUTSIDE AND OFFERS A PRETTY DETAIL WHEN YOU LOOK UP INSIDE THE CANOPY. ▽

△ THE CONSTRUCTION SECRET OF THIS PROJECT IS HIDDEN UNDERNEATH THE ZIGZAG ORGANZA COLLAR: THE OUTER AND INNER HOOPS ARE HELD TOGETHER WITH STAPLES!

# draped canopy

This canopy style is incredibly easy to make and offers lots of design potential. Here, the look is French country with a bold Provençal stripe combined with a smaller paisley print. Create your own mood by using casual seersucker, a textured linen or even sumptuous silk trimmed, respectively, with fantasy fringe, elegant braid or a contrasting fabric band.

## materials

* 3 yd. each of 54"- to 60"-wide coordinating fabrics
* Wall-mounted swing rod that extends approximately 15"
* Wall-mounted curtain tiebacks
* 6 yd. bead trim or other decorative trim (optional)

## instructions

**1** Split each fabric yardage in half widthwise to create two panels.

**2** Pair an outer and lining panel, and stitch together around three sides, leaving one short end open. Trim the seams and corners, turn right-side out and press.

**3** Press under the seam allowance on the open edge and edgestitch the layers closed. Repeat Steps 2 and 3 to assemble the second panel.

**4** If desired, on the outer fabric side, edgestitch the bead trim to one long edge of each assembled panel.

**5** Pin the panels, lining sides together, at one short edge. Follow the Casing with Header instructions on page 112 to measure and sew an appropriately sized rod casing with a 1" to 1½" deep header.

**6** Mount the rod hardware at the desired height and centered above the head of the bed. Thread the rod through the casing, adjust the gathers evenly, and install the rod end in the hardware. Mark the desired swag of each panel on the wall, on either side of the bed, and install the tiebacks. Drape each panel over a tieback, as desired.

IF YOU TIRE OF THE CANOPY'S OUTER FABRIC, CLIP THE CASING STITCHED LINES, REVERSE THE PANELS, AND SEW THE CASING AGAIN. PRESTO! THE LINING FABRIC IS NOW THE PRIMARY PRINT.

# awning canopy

A striped awning canopy transitions this twin bed into guest quarters. The deep red-and-mustard-hued stripes look like a man's necktie and, of course, set the mood. But you can go lighter and brighter with a pretty print or cheerful check for your over-the-bed awning.

## materials

* 54"-wide decorator fabric in the determined yardage
* 2 flat sash rods as long as the canopy finished width, plus mounting hardware
* Gimp trim in the determined yardage (optional)
* Fabric glue

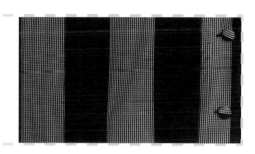

## instructions

**1** To determine the canopy yardage and cutting dimensions, refer to the illustration at right. First, decide on the desired drop behind the headboard (point A). Measure from point A to the ceiling (point B). *Note:* If the ceiling has molding, measure to the molding lower edge. Use a tape measure to create a shallow swag from point B to point C (about 18" to 24" from the wall). Note the tape measure length (swag length).

**2** Use the following formulas to determine the canopy panel cut length, width and required yardage for a self-lined canopy.

| | |
|---|---|
| canopy panel cut length | (distance from point A to point B) + swag length + 13" front flap allowance |
| canopy panel cut width | desired finished width + 1" |
| canopy yardage | (panel cut length x 2) ÷ 36" |
| gimp trim yardage | (canopy yardage x 2) + (canopy panel cut width x 4) ÷ 36" |

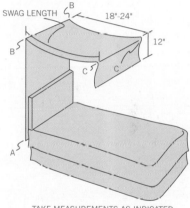

TAKE MEASUREMENTS AS INDICATED.

**1**

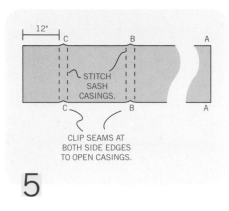

12"

STITCH
SASH
CASINGS.

CLIP SEAMS AT
BOTH SIDE EDGES
TO OPEN CASINGS.

5

**3** Cut two panels in the determined cut width and cut length. Stitch them right sides together around all edges, leaving 12" unstitched on one edge for turning. Trim the seams and corners, turn right-side out and press flat. Press under the seam allowances on the open edge and edgestitch the opening closed.

**4** Glue gimp trim to both sides of the canopy around all edges, if desired.

**5** To create the sash casings, place the assembled canopy on a flat surface. Working from one short end, measure the distance from point A to point B and mark parallel stitching lines across the canopy width for the sash casing. (*Note:* The distance between the lines should be at least 1½" greater than the sash width for threading ease.) Measure 12" from the opposite panel end and mark similar casing stitching lines. Stitch on the marked lines. Use your seam ripper to carefully open the canopy side seams between the stitched casing lines.

**6** Install the casing hardware on the upper wall and ceiling according to the determined canopy measurements. Insert the sash rods through the casings and mount the rods in their hardware.

th the matching Awning Canop
ge 102 and the white Mate
a board cover pictured on page
are the same basic constru
they differ is at their side
e stripe wears buttons and the
atures

*quilted headboard slipcovers*

The striped headboard slipcover shown with the matching Awning Canopy on page 102 and the white Matelassé headboard cover pictured on page 100 share the same basic construction. Where they differ is at their side edges. The stripe wears buttons, and the white features tie closures. Pick your closure and spend an afternoon sewing a new "head" for a bed. *Note*: Instructions are given for slipcovers to cover a twin-size rectangular headboard.

## materials

* ★ 54"- to 60"-wide decorator fabric in the determined yardage
* ★ Backing fabric in the determined yardage
* ★ Low-loft quilt batting
* ★ 5 yd. coordinating ribbon (for the tie-closure slipcover)
* ★ 10 cover buttons, ¾"-diameter and setting tools (for the button-closure slipcover)

## instructions

**1** Measure the headboard width, depth and height. Use the following formulas to determine the panel cut length and width. *Note: The* required yardage for the decorator and backing fabric equals the *panel cut length.*

### Button-Closure Panel Cutting Dimensions

| | |
|---|---|
| panel cut width | headboard width + 6" |
| panel cut length | (headboard height x 2) + headboard depth + 2" |

### Tie-Closure Panel Cutting Dimensions

| | |
|---|---|
| panel cut width | headboard width + 2" |
| panel cut length | (headboard height x 2) + headboard depth + 2" |
| facings | 2½" x panel cut length |

**2** Cut the backing, batting and cover panels in the determined dimensions. *For the tie-closure cover*, also cut two side edge facings.

**3** Follow the Matelassé Coverlet with Zigzag Band instructions beginning on page 80 to layer the cover, batting and backing panels, mark the desired quilting lines, and machine quilt the panel. *Note:* The striped cover is machine-quilted between each stripe.

**4** *To finish the button-closure cover,* fold under and topstitch doubled ½"-deep hems at the cover side edges. Repeat to hem the remaining upper and lower edges.

**5** Place the cover over the headboard, centered and with lower edges aligned. Mark five evenly spaced horizontal buttonhole placements on each side edge. Refer to your machine manual to stitch buttonholes at each mark that are large enough to accommodate the cover buttons.

**6** Cover the buttons with fabric, following the manufacturer's instructions. Sew the buttons along the cover back inside edges to align with the cover front edge buttonholes.

**7** *To finish the tie-closure cover,* place the cover over the headboard, centered and with the lower edges aligned. On the cover front side edges, measure and mark four equally spaced tie placements. Mark corresponding tie placements on the cover back side edges.

**8** Cut the ribbon into 16 ties, approximately 8" to 10" each. Baste a tie end over each placement mark.

**9** Finish one long edge of each facing in a ½"-deep topstitched hem. Stitch a facing long cut edge to each panel side edge, catching the tie ends in the seam.

**10** Turn the facing to the cover wrong side and press the seam flat. Topstitch each cover side edge ½" from the facing seam. Finish the cover lower edges with doubled ½"-deep topstitched hems. Knot the tie ends in overhand knots.

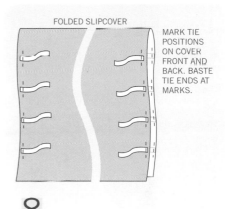

FOLDED SLIPCOVER

MARK TIE POSITIONS ON COVER FRONT AND BACK. BASTE TIE ENDS AT MARKS.

**8**

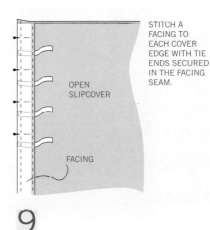

STITCH A FACING TO EACH COVER EDGE WITH TIE ENDS SECURED IN THE FACING SEAM.

OPEN SLIPCOVER

FACING

**9**

Ready-made curtains, especially the sheer and opaque kind, are so inexpensive it doesn't make sense to make them yourself. You can, however, make ready-mades better! Adopt my philosophy of using inexpensive materials lavishly and expensive ones frugally (and wisely). To this end, you can turn basic shirred curtains, like these, into custom treatments with bands of sumptuous silk dupioni. The silk border not only adds style, It can add extra length to the curtains themselves.

## materials

* ★ Purchased pair of lightweight curtain panels in the desired width and equal to or within 12" of the desired length
* ★ 2 yd. 54"-wide dupioni silk (enough for two 12"-deep bands for two curtain panels up to 70" wide)
* ★ Selected curtain rod and mounting hardware

## instructions

**1** Mount the curtain rod at the desired height over the window, and install the curtain panels on the rod. If adding length with the silk bands, measure 11½" up from the floor and mark the curtain panels at this point. If replacing length, pin the curtain panels at the desired finished length, then measure 11½" up from the new hemline and mark the panels.

**2** Remove the panels from the rod. Using the marks made in Step 1, measure and mark each panel across its width and trim the curtains on these marked lines.

**3** To determine the cutting dimensions of the silk bands, measure the width of a curtain panel and add 1"; this is the band cut width. Cut two 25"-deep bands in the determined cut width along the length of the silk fabric (not across the fabric width). *Note:* Cutting the bands lengthwise actually conserves yardage and prevents piecing the band panel if your curtains are wider than the fabric width.

**4** Fold each band in half to measure 12½" deep, and stitch the short edges. Trim the seams and corners, turn right-side out and press the seams flat; also press the band lower edge fold.

**5** Follow the instructions for Attaching Bands on page 173 to sew a band to each curtain panel lower edge.

sew-easy curtain casings

BASIC CASING

MOCK-PLEATED CASING

CASING WITH HEADER

Without rings or pins to attach a curtain to its rod, the curtain itself must have a casing (or channel) through which you insert the curtain rod. Choose your curtain rod first, then consider one of the casing styles presented here as you construct the curtain.

## basic casing

Measure the rod circumference; add 1" to 2" for ease and another ½" for the hem. The resulting figure is the rod casing allowance. This allowance, plus the hem allowance, added to the desired finished length, dictates the curtain panel cutting length. *Note:* The thicker the curtain fabric, the greater the casing ease you will need. Wrap your chosen fabric around the rod, gather it manually and then determine the casing depth. Refer to the illustration below to create the casing.

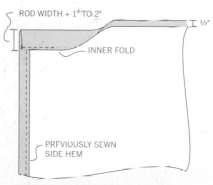

ROD WIDTH + 1" TO 2"  ½"

INNER FOLD

PREVIOUSLY SEWN
SIDE HEM

ON THE CURTAIN PANEL UPPER EDGE, PRESS
UNDER ½" AND THEN PRESS UNDER THE ROD
WIDTH PLUS 1" TO 2". EDGESTITCH CLOSE TO
THE INNER FOLD.

## casing with header

An extra line of stitching across the casing upper edge creates a nice ruffled "header" above the curtain rod. I don't like skimpy headers, so I make mine at least 1" deep. Again, determine the appropriate casing depth to accommodate your rod, add ½" for the lower edge fold, 1" to 2" for ease, and 1" or more for the ruffled header to calculate the total casing/header allowance. Follow the illustration below to sew this casing.

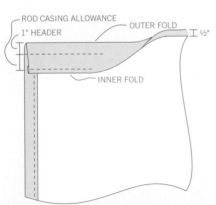

PRESS UNDER ½" AND THEN PRESS UNDER THE CASING/HEADER ALLOWANCE. EDGESTITCH CLOSE TO THE INNER FOLD. TOPSTITCH 1" (OR THE HEADER ALLOWANCE) FROM OUTER FOLD.

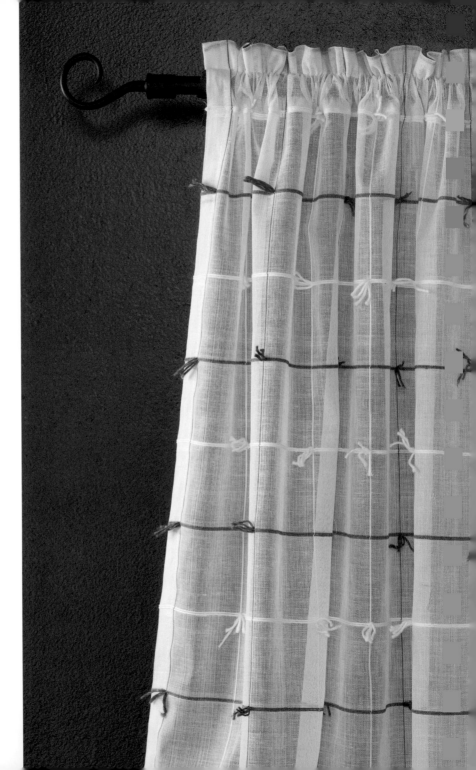

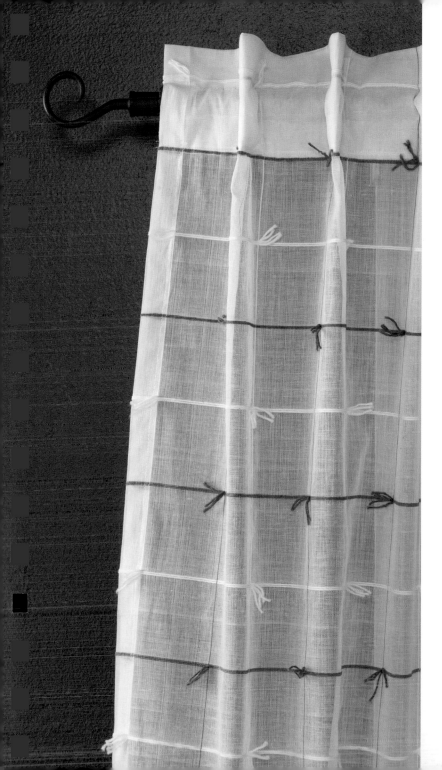

## mock-pleated casing

Equally spaced strips sewn vertically on the curtain header wrong side create the mock pleats on the right side. When calculating the curtain panel cut length, allow 8" for a doubled 4"-deep curtain header. Follow the illustrations below to sew strips to the header wrong side.

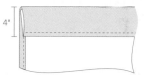

FOLD AND EDGESTITCH A DOUBLED 4"-DEEP HEADER.

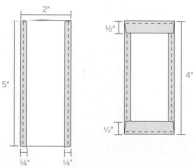

CUT 2½" x 5" STRIPS. EDGESTITCH ¼" HEMS ON LONG EDGES. PRESS UNDER ½" ON SHORT EDGES.

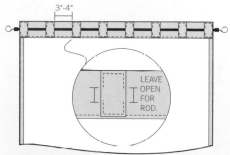

STITCH EVENLY SPACED VERTICAL STRIPS TO HEADER WRONG SIDE AS SHOWN.

# fun stuff for kids and tween

# kids and tweens

Think of the things you can make for your children! The projects here are intended to whet your appetite for years of sewing satisfaction as your family grows. Remember that children learn through your example. The more you sew, the more likely they are to become sewers as well.

I have a confession ... it took nearly 25 years to finish this toy chest. Dave and I carried it into Martha's room with the best of intentions for fabric, paint or stain, but moved it into John's room a few years later still in its original state. Here's my second chance to create the toy chest my children never had, but one that's finally ready (and waiting) for the next generation.

monkey business toy chest

# materials

*Note*: Materials are given to finish the outside and inside of the featured 29½"-wide x 15"-deep x 15½"-high chest with hinged lid and detached top cushion; adjust materials to accommodate your project.

* 4 yd. 54"-wide decorator fabric for the chest outer fabric and seat cushion (*Note*: Indoor/outdoor fabric was used in the featured project, a sensible choice for a child-proof fabrication.)

* 2 yd. 54"-wide coordinating fabric to cover the outer lid and line the chest interior

* 3 yd. each of three coordinating ball fringe trims

* 3 yd. coordinating ribbon wide enough to cover the chest upper edges (optional)

* Twin-size low-loft quilt batting

* 2"-deep upholstery foam slab cut in lid dimensions

* Coordinating craft paint for the chest upper edges and ball feet (optional)

* Large jar of Mod Podge glue/sealant (available in fabric, craft and hobby stores)

* 4 large, unfinished wood knobs and mounting screws for chest "ball feet" (optional)

* Sponge paintbrush (optional)

* Craft knife

* 12" ruler with metal edge

* Staple gun and ⅜" staples

* Fabric glue

* Spray adhesive

* Plastic drop cloth

OPEN THE LID AND SURPRISE! THERE'S A FUN FABRIC LINING INSIDE.

## instructions

**1** To prepare the chest for its fabric re-do, remove the lid and any lid hardware. Pre-drill screw holes for the ball feet if you're using them. Paint the chest upper edges and/or ball feet, as desired, with two or more coats of craft paint. Let the paint dry thoroughly.

**2** Measure the lid, the chest exterior and the chest interior width, depth and height, and note these measurements in the chart below.

### Outer Cover Cutting Dimensions

| | |
|---|---|
| outer cut width | ___" (outer width) + 1" |
| outer cut height | ___" (outer height) + ½" |
| outer cut depth | ___" (outer depth) + 1" |

### Lining Cutting Dimensions

| | |
|---|---|
| interior cut width | ___" (interior width) + 1" |
| interior cut height | ___" (interior height) + ½" |
| interior cut depth | ___" (interior depth) + 1" |

### Lid/Cushion Cutting Dimensions

| | |
|---|---|
| lid/cushion cut width | ___" (lid width) + 1" |
| lid/cushion cut length | ____" (lid depth) + 1" |
| cushion band cut length | ___" (lid perimeter) + 1" |

**3** Refer to the instructions below to cut panels from the outer and lining fabrics.

**From the outer fabric, cut these panels in the determined dimensions**

| | |
|---|---|
| two front/back panels | outer cut width x outer cut height |
| two side panels | outer cut depth x outer cut height |
| one outer bottom panel | outer cut width x outer cut depth |
| lid underside panel | lid cut width x lid cut depth |

**From the lining fabric, cut these panels in the determined dimensions**

| | |
|---|---|
| two inner front/back panels | interior cut width x interior cut height |
| two inner side panels | interior cut depth x interior cut height |
| one inner bottom panel | interior cut width x interior cut depth |
| lid top panel | lid cut width x lid cut length |

**From the outer fabric, cut these panels for the seat cushion**

| | |
|---|---|
| two top/bottom panels | cushion cut width x cushion cut length |
| one cushion band | cushion band cut length x 3" (Cut this band across the fabric width, piecing band lengths, as necessary, to create the required cut length.) |

**4** Lining the chest is much like wallpapering with Mod Podge serving as the paste. Start at the chest interior bottom by applying a generous coat of Mod Podge to this surface. Then center the lining panel on top, smoothing out any bubbles and pressing the excess fabric into edges, corners and up the interior sides. Let the fabric "set" in the glue/sealant for a few minutes. To trim the excess fabric, press the ruler's metal edge into the bottom/side junctures and slice with the craft knife. *Note:* Press hard to make these cuts with one pass of the blade and change blades often.

**5** Repeat the Step 4 instructions to line the chest interior sides and cover the lid top and underside (do not cover the lid edges). If the underside of your lid has bracing bars similar to the featured project, cut extra fabric panels, as necessary; fold the fabric around the brace sides and corners, as if wrapping a present, using Mod Podge as your glue.

**6** To seal these surfaces, apply a final light topcoat of Mod Podge with special concentration at the fabric cut edges to prevent them from raveling. Let the chest and lid dry overnight.

**7** To pad the chest, cover your work surface with a plastic drop cloth and place the chest upside-down on top. Insert small wood blocks or other objects under the chest corners to raise it slightly. Unfold the quilt batting and loosely wrap it around the chest sides; trim some excess batting to create a more manageable piece. Liberally spray one chest side with adhesive and immediately press the batting onto this surface. Repeat to cover all sides of the chest, butting the batting edges at one chest corner. Trim the batting flush with the chest upper and lower edges.

**8** Follow the Box-edge Corners instructions beginning on page 178 to assemble the chest outer fabric cover. *Note:* This "box" resembles the Tissue Box Cover on page 71.

**9** Slide the outer cover over the padded chest, pull its edges flush with the chest upper edges, and staple ½" below the chest edges. Trim ¼" of batting from under the cover fabric above the staples, and glue the cover edge to the chest.

**10** Follow the Box-Edge Cushion Cover instructions on page 179 to assemble the seat cushion. Glue one row of ball fringe around the cushion band lower edge.

**11** To finish, attach the ball knob feet, and reattach the lid. Glue one row of ball fringe around the lid edge, and another row of fringe around the chest upper edge. Glue ribbon over the chest upper edges, as desired.

*growth chart*

Instead of notching your woodwork, record your child's growth milestones with a fabric marker on this appliquéd chart. Once he or she grows "off the chart," you can roll up this keepsake and save it as a point of reference for future disputes about who was taller ... and when.

## materials

* 1 yd. 54"-wide woven check fabric (*Note*: Make sure to select a check with an even pattern that's easy to measure and mark the inches.)
* Print fabric with large motifs in sufficient yardage to provide 10 to 12 cutouts
* 2 yd. heavy-weight fusible web
* ¾"-diameter dowel rod cut into two 13" lengths for the chart upper and lower supports
* Squeeze-bottle dimensional paint in a coordinating color to mark the chart's inches
* Chenille trim or ribbon for the chart's foot marks
* 4 wood knobs to cover the dowel ends
* Coordinating craft paint to paint the dowel rods and knobs
* Sponge paintbrush
* Wood glue

## instructions

**1** Cut two 12" x 48" panels (across the fabric width) from the check fabric. Follow the fusible web manufacturer's instructions to fuse these panels, right sides together.

**2** Follow the Cutting and Applying Bias Binding instructions on page 180 to bind the fused panel long side edges with ½"-wide bias made from the check fabric.

**3** To make the dowel rod casings, press under ¼", then 1¾" on each panel short edge. Topstitch ¼" from the inner fold of each casing.

**4** Adhere fusible web to the wrong side of the print fabric and under the desired motifs. Use very sharp scissors with short blades to carefully cut out the fused print motifs. Peel off the web paper backing, arrange the motifs as desired along the long left edge of the chart and fuse.

**5** Place the chart, right-side up, on a flat surface. Start at the lower casing right edge fold and use tailor's chalk to mark 1" increments, horizontally, up the chart's right edge. The first inch mark should designate either 1-foot 9" or 1-foot 10". Paint these vertical lines with the squeeze bottle dimensional paint and let dry overnight.

**6** Cut and stitch chenille trim in the shape of numbers to designate the 2-foot, 3-foot, 4-foot and 5-foot heights along the chart right edge, as well as the exact foot mark for each with short chenille strips stitched over the corresponding inch marks.

**7** To finish, paint the dowels and knobs with several coats of craft paint and let them dry thoroughly. Slide a dowel through each casing and glue the knobs to the dowel ends. Hang the chart, measuring up from the floor to coincide with the chart's first marked inch.

Who knew that the '60s hot pink and orange would cycle back into vogue? Yet, here they are again as primary colors in home décor accessories and retro printed fabrics. Hipster that I am, I dug out the real thing from my fabric stash in the form of a linen tablecloth (circa 1964) for these projects. Madeleine has ear-marked both for her cherry pink bedroom.

## materials

* Photo album
* Fabric in the yardage equal to the album height + 6"
* Medium-weight fusible interfacing
* Flat button
* Pair of Velcro squares or dots
* Fabric glue
* Spray adhesive

To make a skirted shelf like this one, follow the *Make Me Blush* Shelf instructions on page 69. Instead of gimp, use a double layer of funky beaded trim, with one layer stapled to the shelf edge, upside down, and the second glued over the skirt upper edge. With a little coaxing, the bead strands of the first layer can be trained to hang over the skirt.

# instructions

**1** Cut a fabric panel 6" wider and 6" longer than the open album cover dimensions. Fuse the interfacing to the wrong side of the fabric panel.

**2** Place the panel wrong-side up on a flat surface. Open the album and place it, outer side down, on top of the panel. Center the album within the panel, and then trace its shape. Add 2" to each traced edge and cut out the cover panel. Turn under and topstitch a ½"-deep hem on each cover panel edge.

**3** Cut a 2"-wide tab long enough to wrap from the album back edge to front edge (assuming a full album), plus 6". Press under ¼" on the tab edges, fold the tab in half widthwise, and edgestitch the entire tab. Fold under 1" on one tab end and edgestitch.

**4** Use your machine to stitch the button on the right side of this tab end. Refer to the illustration at right to attach the tab to the cover panel back edge.

**5** Place the cover panel wrong-side up on a flat, protected surface, and liberally spray it with adhesive. Place the open album cover centered on top, and press into the adhesive. Fold the excess cover fabric to the album inside edges and glue.

**6** To make a fabric photo frame for the cover front, cut a fabric square or rectangle 2" larger than the size of the desired photo; fuse interfacing to its wrong side. Press under ½" on each edge and edgestitch.

**7** Draw the photo dimensions in the center of the interfaced side of the frame fabric. Stitch ⅛" inside these drawn lines. Slit the interior of this stitched area, turn the excess fabric to the frame wrong side and press well. Trim the excess interior fabric to ½" and edgestitch the opening.

**8** Glue the frame to the album cover front leaving one edge open for photo insertion. Glue a Velcro loop square or dot to the underside of the tab end. Glue the corresponding hook square or dot to the album front.

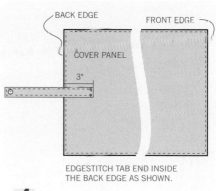

EDGESTITCH TAB END INSIDE THE BACK EDGE AS SHOWN.

**4**

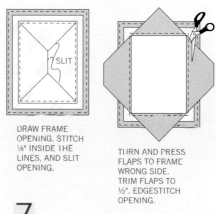

DRAW FRAME OPENING. STITCH ⅛" INSIDE THE LINES, AND SLIT OPENING.

TURN AND PRESS FLAPS TO FRAME WRONG SIDE. TRIM FLAPS TO ½". EDGESTITCH OPENING.

**7**

Make one, make a dozen, in different fabrics, with buckled straps or without. This very versatile tote can be sized up or down to accommodate many needs, such as a day at the beach. A bag, a towel, some flip flops ... what more does she need? (P.S.: Mom, slip in some sunscreen and your work is done!)

tote bag

## materials

* ⅔ yd. each of two coordinating medium-weight cotton canvas fabrics
* Medium-weight fusible interfacing
* 2 pairs of 1"-wide purse buckles (optional)

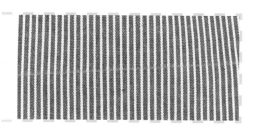

## instructions

**1** Fuse interfacing to the wrong side of each fabric. *Note:* This interfacing adds body and structure to the tote.

**2** Cut two 17" x 15" panels and two 2" x 36" handle strips from each interfaced fabric. *Note:* Use one pair of panels and strips in the same fabric as the tote outer fabric, and the second set as the tote/strap lining.

**3** Stitch the outer panels around three sides, leaving one 15" edge open. Stitch the lining panels together around the same three sides, but leave approximately 4" unstitched in the center of one 15" edge. *Note:* This opening will be used later for turning.

**4** Fold the outer and lining panel corners into triangles with the side seam centered; draw 4"-long stitching lines perpendicular to the seams, and stitch. Trim the excess triangles. *Note:* The stitched corners create the tote's 4" depth. Adjust the corner folds and length of the stitched line to create more or less depth, as desired.

**5** To make the tote straps, pair an outer fabric and lining strip and stitch the long edges. Trim the seams, turn right side out and press. Edgestitch the strap edges.

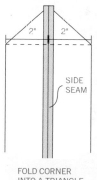

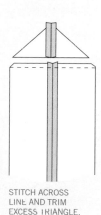

2" 2"

SIDE SEAM

FOLD CORNER INTO A TRIANGLE AND MARK 4" STITCHING LINE PERPENDICULAR TO THE CENTERED SIDE SEAM.

STITCH ACROSS LINE AND TRIM EXCESS TRIANGLE.

**4**

RAW EDGES

1½"

LOOP EACH TAB.

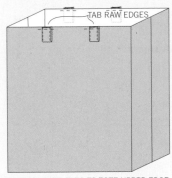

TAB RAW EDGES

BASTE LOOPED TABS TO TOTE UPPER EDGE.

OR

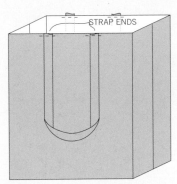

STRAP ENDS

BASTE STRAP ENDS TO TOTE UPPER EDGE.

6

**6** Trim two 3"-long tabs from each strap. Fold each tab in half to create a 1½" loop; baste the loop edges to the outer tote upper edge as shown. *Note:* If you're not using purse buckles, trim the straps to the desired length and stitch the ends to the tote upper edge.

**7** Turn the tote lining wrong-side out. Insert the outer tote inside the lining, right sides together, with their upper edges and seams aligned; pin. *Note:* The loop ends (or strap ends) should be sandwiched between these layers. Stitch around the tote/lining upper edge.

**8** Turn the lining/tote right-side out through the lining lower edge opening. Fold under the lining seam allowances and whipstitch them closed.

**9** Fold the lining inside the tote, press the upper edge seam flat and edgestitch. Treat the two layers as one and press sharp creases along the tote side and bottom edges to reinforce its box shape; edgestitch all creased lines catching the lining fabric in the stitches.

**10** Follow the buckle manufacturer's instructions to insert/attach the flat end of a buckle through each loop. Loop the strap ends through the buckles, turn under ½" on the handle ends and topstitch to secure the straps to the buckles.

## flower power

Heavy-weight fusible web comes in handy for lots of sewing projects, like this multi-layered flower. To make a similar fabric flower, fuse two layers of selected fabrics, wrong sides together. Cut out desired petal shapes and stack them. Use your machine to sew a button in the center through all layers, and a safety pin to secure this bit of flower power to a hat or garment.

Elaborate window treatments in the baby's nursery? It just doesn't make sense when the child grows up — fast — and all too soon yesterday's beloved pastels don't appeal to the emerging teen. Instead, make a modest short-term investment, in both time and materials costs, to create this whimsical valance (with companion organdy café curtain) using, of all things, placemats!

pleated placemat valance

## materials

- ★ Purchased placemats
- ★ Flat curtain rod for the valance
- ★ Remnant fabric for the rod casing
- ★ Trim for the purchased café curtains in yardage equal to the curtain finished width

## instructions

**1** The featured valance is made from lined placemats with printed motifs and borders. To keep the borders intact, it's best to adapt the valance finished width by modifying the depth of the pleats. With this in mind, determine the number of placemats needed for your valance, allowing 4" to 8" for each pleat between the joined mats.

**2** Edgestitch the mats, side edge to side edge; open the mats and press these "seams" flat. At each seam upper edge, form inverted pleats of the desired depth and press. Baste the pleat upper edges.

**3** Cut and piece, as necessary, a rod casing strip from remnant fabric that is 1" longer than the valance finished width and 1" to 2" deeper than the rod width.

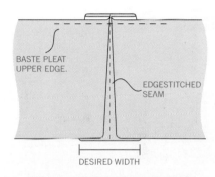

BASTE PLEAT UPPER EDGE.

EDGESTITCHED SEAM

DESIRED WIDTH

FORM AN INVERTED PLEAT OF THE DESIRED DEPTH AT EACH EDGESTITCHED SEAM.

**2**

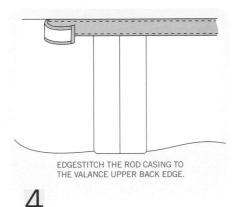

EDGESTITCH THE ROD CASING TO
THE VALANCE UPPER BACK EDGE.

**4**

**4** Press under ½" on the casing strip short edges, and ¼" on the casing long edges. Pin the casing across the upper back edge of the valance, and edgestitch the long edges.

**5** Thread the rod through the valance casing, and hang the valance.

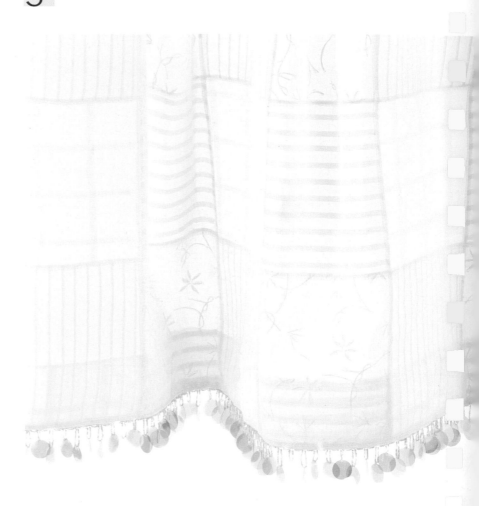

EDGESTITCH THE HEADER OF A FANTASY TRIM TO THE UNDERSIDE OF THE CURTAIN HEM SO THAT JUST THE TRIM DANGLES BELOW. JUST MAKE SURE THIS FASCINATING TRIM HANGS ABOVE THE REACH OF CURIOUS LITTLE FINGERS.

Whether it's Go Fish or Texas Hold 'Em, you've got it covered with this fitted felt table topper. The only requirement is a table with a lip to hold the topper's elastic-encased edge. The optional darker green top panel helps "define" the card-playing area. Use wool (or wool/blend) felt instead of an acrylic felt ... you'll appreciate the touch and weight of your topper so much more.

## materials

★ Wool felt panel equal to table top width + 8" x table top length + 8" (*Note*: Wool felt is available in varying widths. A 54"- to 60"-wide felt will be more expensive than narrower yardage, but you'll get more bang for your buck with the extra width.)

★ Coordinating wool felt panel equal to table top width x table top length for the inner panel (optional)

★ 1"-wide elastic in yardage equal to the table top perimeter

★ Spray adhesive (optional)

★ Round plate or cup

## instructions

*Note*: The featured table is 32" wide and 48" long. Its topper required a little over 1 yard of 60"-wide felt because the felt width was used for the topper length.

1 Trace around a plate or cup at each topper panel corner, and cut on the traced lines to curve the corners.

2 If using a coordinating inner panel, trim it 2" to 4" smaller than the length and width of the table top. Mark this panel's placement on the topper panel right side (i.e. centered side-to-side and top-to-bottom). Spray a liberal amount of adhesive on the inner panel wrong side and adhere it to the topper panel within the placement lines. Let the adhesive dry for 30 minutes, and then topstitch the coordinating panel about ½" from its edges.

3 Fold under and edgestitch a 1½"-deep elastic casing around the topper panel edges; leave 3" to 4" unstitched for elastic insertion.

4 Use a bodkin or large safety pin to thread the elastic through the casing. Pull the elastic to gather the topper edges, and test-fit the topper on your table. Adjust the elastic until you achieve a snug fit. Overlap the elastic and stitch across it several times for a secure joining. Trim the excess elastic. Tuck the elastic inside the casing and edgestitch the casing opening closed.

When Jennie says "I need to pick your brain," I immediately head to the sewing machine ... for a very good cause. Jennie is director of a local not-for-profit organization that fights child abuse through many programs. For over 20 years, this organization has run a children's holiday store (*Stocking Stuffers*) where kids can buy great, inexpensive gifts. These 3-foot long stockings are the result of one of Jennie's brain-picking sessions, and I'm proud to say they've hung outside the *Stocking Stuffers* shop for several seasons.

Making your own "custom" felt stockings is easy ... forget patterns, use your imagination, and follow these design tips:

- Wool felt is an excellent stocking material. It doesn't ravel, looks good on both sides, is easy to sew, and comes in wonderful colors. My stocking palette was olive green, ruby red and soft white. Yours could be purple, orange and fuchsia!

- Experiment with different stocking shapes, long and skinny, short and wide, pointy toed, etc. If making more than one stocking, draw and cut a muslin pattern.

- The polka dots on the red stockings are simply tracings of a cup, saucer and salad plate from my everyday dishes. You can use cookie cutters to trace stars, or stencils to trace letters, numbers or other interesting shapes.

- Take a walk down the crafting aisle of a fabric store ... you'll find pom poms (for a snowman's buttons), chenille stems (for skis) and other fun stuff (cutout snowflakes) plus tools to give your stocking motifs more detail. (*Note:* I used a hole punch to punch out the snowman's eyes.)

- Once you've finished decorating your stocking front, sew the front and back stocking panels together using a ⅝" seam. Then use pinking shears to trim ¼" from this meant-to-be-seen seam allowance.

# family affair

# family affair

The rec room is the final resting place for castoff furniture, along with the toys, video games, extra TV and other room remainders. This catchall room is where you and your children spend important time, and it could probably use some updating. Consider adapting the following projects to marry up your mismatched furniture, add comforting pillows, create a classy cover-up for the "media center," and provide storage for the always-missing remote controls.

This secondhand chair with teak frame was in good shape overall, but the cushion fabric was very sad. It took just one afternoon to sew new covers in this interesting geometric print. Pretty cool, huh? You, too, can resurrect an old chair with good bones by making new cushion covers ... just follow this basic construction technique.

box-edge cushion covers

## materials

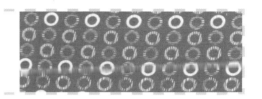

* 54" wide decorator fabric in determined yardage
* Pattern tracing cloth or muslin (if needed)

## instructions

**1** To determine the cutting dimensions of one cushion cover, take these measurements, adding 1" to each for seam allowances, and write them in the chart below:

cushion width at is widest point for the top/bottom panel +1"    _____

cushion length at its longest point for the top/bottom panel +1"    _____

cushion depth for the box band +1"    _____

cushion circumference for the box band +1"    _____

**2** Follow the Drawing a Sample Cutting Layout instructions on page 187 to sketch a layout and determine the required yardage for two top/bottom panels and one box band.

**3** If your cushion is exactly square or rectangular, use the measurements taken in Step 1 to cut all panels. If the cushion is irregularly shaped (as are both of the featured cushions), make a pattern by placing the tracing cloth or muslin over the cushion top and carefully tracing its shape. Draw the cutting lines ½" beyond the traced lines. Use this pattern to cut out the top/bottom panels; use the dimensions determined in Step 1 to cut out the box band, cutting several strips as necessary to achieve the required length.

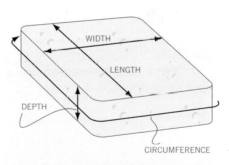

MEASURE CUSHION AT ITS WIDEST POINTS.

1

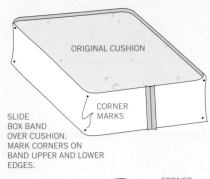

ORIGINAL CUSHION

CORNER MARKS

SLIDE BOX BAND OVER CUSHION. MARK CORNERS ON BAND UPPER AND LOWER EDGES.

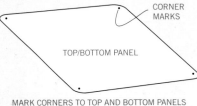

CORNER MARKS

TOP/BOTTOM PANEL

MARK CORNERS TO TOP AND BOTTOM PANELS

**4**

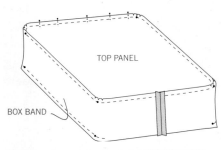

TOP PANEL

BOX BAND

PIN TOP PANEL TO BAND, ALIGNING CORNER MARKS. STITCH.

**5**

**4** To assemble the cover, stitch the box band short edges and press the seam open.

**5** Follow the Box-Edge Corners instructions beginning on page 178 to stitch the top and bottom panels to the band edges, leaving one bottom panel/band edge unstitched. Turn the cover right-side out.

**6** Insert the cushion inside its new cover. Fold under the seam allowances on the cover open edges and slipstitch the opening closed.

An easy chair needs an ottoman, so I went shopping at my favorite "gently used" consignment store. I found one in the right shape and size, but in definite need of a new outfit. Instead of ignoring its semi-attached top cushion with a cube-like cover-up, I opted for mock-box corners on top and a tailored box-pleated skirt on the bottom. My bargain find was now a well-dressed gal. All she needed was the right accessory ... a simple D-ring belt.

*rehabbed ottoman*

## materials

* ★ Square or rectangular ottoman with semi-attached top
* ★ 54"-wide decorator fabric in determined yardage
* ★ Low-loft batting in dimensions equal to top panel cutting dimensions
* ★ 2 "D" rings, 1¼"-wide (optional)
* ★ 1"- to 1¼"-wide grosgrain ribbon in yardage equal to twice the ottoman circumference + 8" (optional)

## instructions

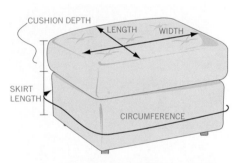

MEASURE CUSHION WIDTH, LENGTH AND DEPTH, OTTOMAN CIRCUMFERENCE AND SKIRT LENGTH AS SHOWN.

1

1 To determine the cutting dimensions of your ottoman slipcover, take the following measurements and write them in the chart below:

| | |
|---|---|
| cushion top width | ___ |
| cushion top length | ___ |
| cushion top depth | ___ |
| ottoman circumference where the skirt will be attached | ___ |
| skirt length to the floor | ___ |

**Determine the slipcover top panel cutting dimensions:**

| | |
|---|---|
| width + (depth x 2) + 1" x<br>length + (depth x 2) + 1" | ___ x ___ |

**Determine the skirt cutting dimensions:**

| | |
|---|---|
| circumference + 25" (24" pleat allowance + 1" seam allowance) | skirt width |
| skirt length + 4½" (4" hem allowance + ½" seam allowance) | skirt length |

**2** To determine the required yardage, follow the instructions for Drawing a Sample Cutting Layout on page 187 and use the panel cutting dimensions determined in Step 1 to sketch a layout and determine the required yardage for two top panels (one used for lining) and one skirt panel.

**3** Cut out the top and skirt panels. Also cut a batting panel in the same dimensions as the top panel. Baste the batting panel to the top panel wrong side around all edges.

**4** Center the top panel, fabric-side down, on the ottoman top. Pin the corners as shown to create a snug fit and mark a stitching line at each corner. Repeat to pin-fit and mark the top lining. Stitch the corners, trim the excess fabric and press.

**5** Stitch the short ends of the skirt panel and press the seam open. On the skirt lower edge press under a double 2"-deep hem and topstitch close to the hem inner fold.

**6** Place the skirt over the ottoman and pin-fit a 3"-wide box pleat at each corner, being careful to conceal the skirt seam inside one pleat. Remove the skirt and baste across each pleat upper edge.

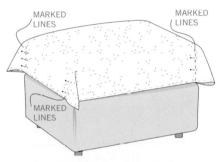

MARKED LINES    MARKED LINES

MARKED LINES

PIN-FIT TOP PANEL TO OTTOMAN CUSHION. MARK CORNER STITCHING LINES.

**4**

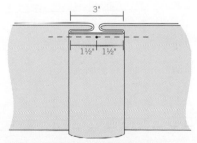

3"

1½"  1½"

FORM 3"-WIDE BOX PLEAT AT EACH OTTOMAN CORNER. BASTE THE PLEAT UPPER EDGE.

**6**

**7** Pin the skirt upper edge to the top panel, making sure to position each top panel corner in the center of its corresponding pleat. (*Note:* As a result of this pinning, the skirt will be folded into the top panel.) Baste the skirt to the top panel around all edges, being careful not to catch the skirt fabric in the seam.

**8** With the skirt sandwiched in between, pin the lining panel to the top panel and stitch together around three edges, leaving one edge unstitched for turning.

**9** Turn the slipcover right-side out through the top panel opening, releasing the skirt in the process. Fold under the seam allowances on the top panel/lining open edge and slipstitch the opening closed.

**10** To make the optional ribbon belt, press under ½" on both ends of the ribbon length. Fold the ribbon in half and edgestitch all edges. Insert one ribbon end through both D-rings, form a tight loop and stitch the ribbon layers close to the ring flat edges. Tie the belt around the slipcovered ottoman over the top/skirt seam.

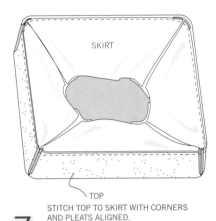

SKIRT

TOP

STITCH TOP TO SKIRT WITH CORNERS AND PLEATS ALIGNED.

**7**

## slip into something better

Slipcover making is like garment making in a sense ... both involve fitting fabric to cover a specific object, be it the arm of a chair or the arm of a person. When you're ready to take on a more involved slipcover project, I recommend consulting sewing books on this subject and examining commercially-made slipcovers for details and ideas for your own project. For a cover that goes over existing upholstery, your job is to replicate, as necessary, the upholstery seams and fitting detail. This is what I did with this chair that now wears a new denim overcoat with two add-ons: a seat cushion and a short flat skirt. The one-piece cover slips over the chair (no zipper or other opening) and the little bit of extra fabric (ease) gets tucked into the seat crevices. Smooth the skirt, put the cushion on the seat, and it's a whole new chair.

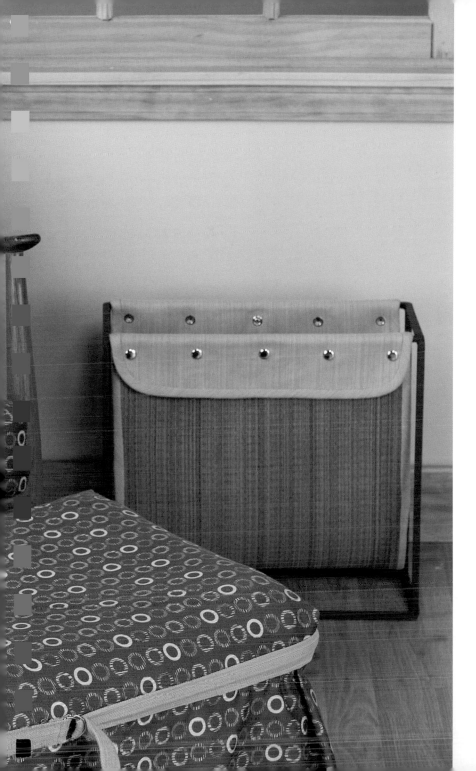

## magazine caddy

This metal frame once had leather straps and was used as a kindling/log holder. To change its function from wood to the printed page, I cut off the straps and substituted a fabric panel made from two companion fabrics fused wrong sides together. After binding the panel edges with bias made from one of the panel fabrics (see the technique on page 180), I looped the panel ends over the frame upper supports to mark the location of five nickel-colored snaps. (*Note:* Dritz sells a wide array of snaps and setting tools in retail fabric and hobby stores; see the Resources on page 188.) Once installed, the snaps secure the panel to the frame. Keep an eye open for an odd container or frame, like this one, and fill in its "blanks" with fabric.

media center

If you hate the standard black laminate TV cabinet — but don't want to invest in a pricey unit for the rec room — here's an affordable alternative: a basic shelving unit with a slipcover! The one shown here features a Velcro front closure, mock-paneled door fronts outlined in grosgrain ribbon, and a separate topper that hides more Velcro securing the cover to the shelf. Think beyond your media needs to adapt this storage concept for a bedroom armoire, a deluxe cabinet for the home office, or a pretty sewing center for your hobby room.

## materials

* Shelving unit (*Note*: Select a unit with at least a 1"-deep flat upper edge to hold the self-adhesive Velcro hook tape.)
* Outer and lining fabrics in the determined yardage
* Sew-in Velcro tape (hook and loop sections) in the determined yardage
* 1"-wide self-adhesive Velcro hook tape in yardage equal to the shelf perimeter
* Fabric glue
* 2 large buttons (optional)
* 1"-wide grosgrain ribbon (optional)
* Fusible seam tape (optional)
* Spray paint in desired color

## instructions

1 Assemble the shelving unit. If desired, spray paint all interior surfaces in a desired color to make it look finished when the door flaps are open. Measure the unit's width, height, depth, and perimeter.

2 Add 1" to each measurement taken in Step 1 and use these adjusted measurements in the chart on the following page to determine the cutting dimensions of the cover panels.

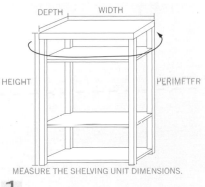

MEASURE THE SHELVING UNIT DIMENSIONS.

1

| back panel cutting dimensions | ____" (width) x ____" (height) | cut one each from outer and lining fabrics |
|---|---|---|
| side panel cutting dimensions | ____" (depth) x ____" (height) | cut two each from outer and lining fabrics |
| front panel cutting dimensions | ___" (width ÷ 2) + 2½" x ____" (height) | cut two each from outer and lining fabrics |
| topper panel | ____" (width) x ____" (depth) | cut one from outer fabric |
| cover and topper skirts | ____" (perimeter + 30") x 8" | cut two from outer fabric, piecing panels end-to-end as necessary to create the required cut length |
| 1"-wide self-adhesive Velcro hook tape and corresponding sew-in loop tape | ____" (perimeter) | cut in length indicated |
| sew-in Velcro hook and loop tape | ____" (height) + 12" | cut in length indicated |

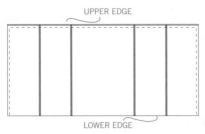

UPPER EDGE

LOWER EDGE

AFTER ASSEMBLING OUTER AND LINING PANELS SEPARATELY, STITCH THEM TOGETHER AS SHOWN. LEAVE LOWER EDGE OPEN.

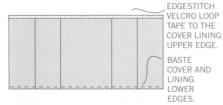

EDGESTITCH VELCRO LOOP TAPE TO THE COVER LINING UPPER EDGE.

BASTE COVER AND LINING LOWER EDGES.

**5**

**3** Use the cutting dimensions in the chart above and follow the Drawing a Sample Cutting Layout instructions on page 187 to sketch a layout and determine the required outer fabric and lining yardages. Cut all required fabric panels.

**4** Assemble the outer cover and the lining panels separately, and then assemble the outer cover and the lining. Trim seams and corners, turn right-side out, and press.

**5** Baste the cover lower edges. Edgestitch the 1"-wide sew-in Velcro loop tape to the cover upper edge on the lining side.

WITH THE FRONT PANELS OPEN, THE "CABINET" REVEALS A TV, DVD PLAYER AND STORAGE FOR MOVIES AND VIDEO GAMES.

**6** Adhere the 1"-wide self-adhesive Velcro hook tape around the shelf upper edge. With cover seams matching shelf corners, adhere the cover upper edge to the shelf upper edge. Overlap and pin the front panels to close the cover. Mark the vertical overlap edge on the lower panel. Remove the cover, cut and then stitch Velcro hook tape to the left front panel with the tape edge just inside the marked line as shown. Stitch the corresponding Velcro loop tape to the lining side of the right front panel.

**7** Cut and stitch the remaining sew-in Velcro tape sections to the front panel upper edges to secure them to the cover side panels when the cover is open.

**8** To make the cover skirt, fold the skirt panel in half widthwise and stitch the short ends. Trim the seams and corners, turn the panel right-side out and press the lower edge fold. Baste the upper cut edges.

**9** Reattach the cover to the shelving unit and close the front panels. Pin-fit the skirt around the cover lower edge, forming 3"-wide inverted pleats at the cover seam/shelf corners. Also measure and mark the skirt stitching line around the cover lower edge so that the skirt, when attached, will just brush the floor. Trim the excess cover ½" below this marked line.

**10** Remove the skirt and baste the pleated upper edges. Remove the cover and follow the Attaching Bands instructions beginning on page 173 to attach and finish the skirt.

**11** To make the topper, follow the Step 8 instructions to prepare the topper skirt panel. Pin-fit the skirt panel around the topper edges, forming five 3"-wide inverted pleats, one at each topper corner and the fifth at the topper center front. Follow the Step 9 and 10 instructions to attach the skirt and finish the topper.

**12** If desired, create mock inset panels on the cover front panels with grosgrain ribbon, positioning the ribbon first with fusible seam tape followed by edgestitching; add edgestitched ribbon to outline the front panel overlapped edges. Sew buttons to the front panel overlapped edges as mock "door knobs" if desired.

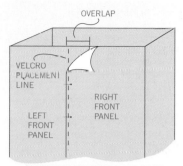

OVERLAP FRONT PANELS AND MARK VELCRO PLACEMENT LINE.

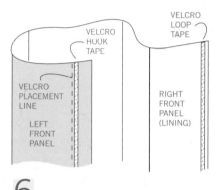

**6**

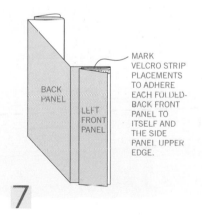

MARK VELCRO STRIP PLACEMENTS TO ADHERE EACH FOLDED-BACK FRONT PANEL TO ITSELF AND THE SIDE PANEL UPPER EDGE.

**7**

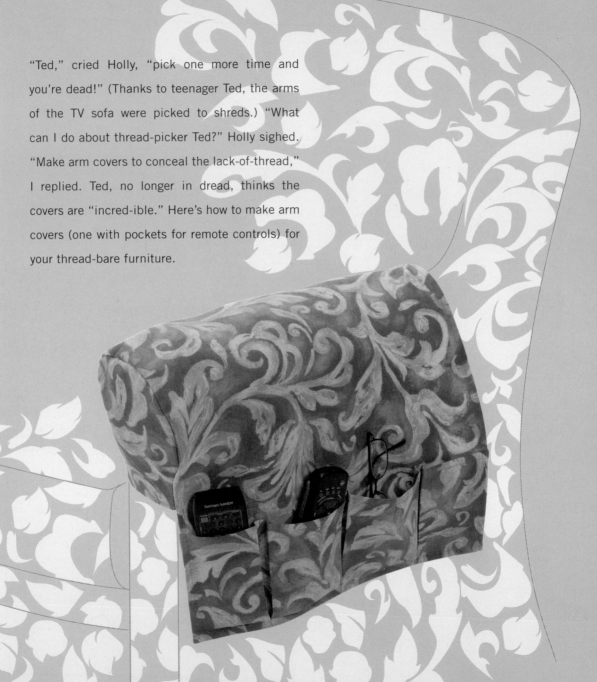

"Ted," cried Holly, "pick one more time and you're dead!" (Thanks to teenager Ted, the arms of the TV sofa were picked to shreds.) "What can I do about thread-picker Ted?" Holly sighed. "Make arm covers to conceal the lack-of-thread," I replied. Ted, no longer in dread, thinks the covers are "incred-ible." Here's how to make arm covers (one with pockets for remote controls) for your thread-bare furniture.

*arm covers*

## materials

* ★ ½ to 1 yd. 54"-wide decorator fabric that matches or coordinates with your chair or sofa fabric
* ★ Leftover interfacing, lightweight fabric or pattern tracing cloth

## instructions

**1** Use the interfacing, fabric or tracing cloth to trace and cut the arm front panel pattern, adding ½" to all edges as shown. Use this pattern to cut one arm front from the fabric.

**2** Use a tape measure to measure the curved edge of the arm front panel. This measurement is the *panel length*. Measure the arm depth and add ½"; this is the *panel width*. Determine the extra inches desired for the pockets; this is the *pocket allowance*. Use these measurements to cut the arm panel from the fabric, and to mark and clip the seam allowance at the front edge as shown.

TRACE ARM FRONT AND THEN ADD ½" TO ALL EDGES.

USE TRACING TO CUT ARM FRONT FROM FABRIC.

**1**

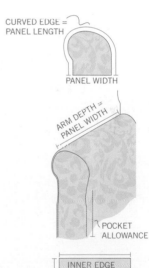

CURVED EDGE = PANEL LENGTH

PANEL WIDTH

ARM DEPTH = PANEL WIDTH

POCKET ALLOWANCE

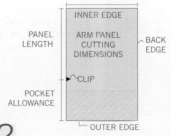

INNER EDGE

PANEL LENGTH

ARM PANEL CUTTING DIMENSIONS

BACK EDGE

CLIP

POCKET ALLOWANCE

OUTER EDGE

**2**

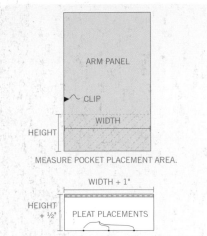

ARM PANEL

CLIP

WIDTH

HEIGHT

MEASURE POCKET PLACEMENT AREA.

WIDTH + 1"

HEIGHT + ½"

PLEAT PLACEMENTS

USE MEASUREMENTS TO DRAW AND CUT POCKET PANEL.
FINISH UPPER EDGE WITH A ½" TOPSTITCHED HEM.
MARK THREE EVENLY SPACED PLEATS ON LOWER EDGE.

3

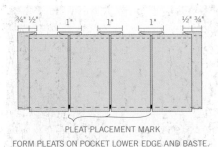

¾" ½"   1"   1"   1"   ½" ¾"

PLEAT PLACEMENT MARK

FORM PLEATS ON POCKET LOWER EDGE AND BASTE.

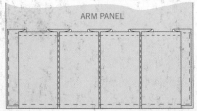

ARM PANEL

BASTE POCKET PANEL TO ARM PANEL AROUND
POCKET EDGES. TOPSTITCH BETWEEN PLEATS TO
CREATE INDIVIDUAL POCKETS.

4

3 Use the pocket placement area dimensions to cut the pocket panel, finish its upper edge with a ½" topstitched hem, and mark pleat locations on its lower edge as shown.

4 On the pocket panel lower edge, create inverted pleats at each pleat placement mark, and partial pleats at the pocket panel side edges; baste the pocket panel lower edge to secure the pleats. Baste the pocket panel to the arm panel lower edge as shown. Stitch vertically between the pleat folds to create the individual pockets.

5 Clean-finish, press under and topstitch ½"-deep hems on all edges of the arm panel except the front edge above the clip. Also, clean-finish, press under and topstitch a ½"-deep hem on the arm front lower edge.

6 To assemble the arm front and arm/pocket panel, pin then stitch the arm front curved edge to the arm panel front edge above the clip, following the Joining Curved and Straight Edges instructions on page 183. Trim and clean-finish the seam allowance.

*basic arm cover*

If pockets aren't your priority, but protecting the fabric on the arms of your furniture is, just follow Steps 1, 2 (omitting extra inches for the pocket allowance), 5 and 6 of the instructions above to make the basic arm cover.

floor pillow

Knife-edge pillow construction calls for cutting front and back panels 1" larger than the pillow form dimensions. This makes sense in theory, but through experience I know that pillow forms are limp at the corners. To plump up these corners, I add a little fiberfill to the pillow cover corners before stitching the cover closed. Try this yourself and you'll be pleased with the results.

## materials

* ★ 24" x 24" pillow form
* ★ ¾ yd. 54"-wide decorator fabric
* ★ 3 yd. decorative sew-in trim
* • Polyester fiberfill

## cutting instructions

From the decorator fabric, cut:
* ★ Two 25" x 25" panels

## instructions

BASTE THE TRIM WOVEN EDGES AROUND THE EDGES OF ONE PILLOW PANEL, BUTTING THE TRIM CUT EDGES.

1

**1** Baste the decorative trim around the edges of one panel using a ⅜" seam.

**2** Stitch the two panels right sides together around all sides, but leave about 15" unstitched on one edge. Turn the cover right-side out through this opening. In lieu of pressing (which may damage your trim), gently pull the trim ends to fully open the cover seams.

**3** Stuff a handful or two of fiberfill into the cover corners before inserting the pillow form. Add more or remove some fiberfill as desired. Fold under the seam allowances on the opening edges and slipstitch the opening closed.

John studied the buckles on this pillow and gave me a puzzled look. "But they don't unbuckle anything," he said. Dave piped in with his opinion, too: "Those buckles will dig into my back." I turned the pillow over to reveal its plain side. "Oh," they said in unison. In my view, all form does not have to function, and buckles provide interesting detail. Hardware meets software. Just for fun. Get it? If not, turn the pillow over.

buckled pillow

## materials

- ★ 20" x 14" pillow form
- ★ 3 coordinating fabrics:
  - • ½ yd. primary fabric
  - • ¼ yd. band fabric
  - • Fabric leftovers for buckle loops
- ★ 3 swivel-ring buckles with spring clasps, similar to a leash buckle, 2"-long (available in the purse-making notions area of fabric and craft stores)
- ★ Polyester fiberfill

## cutting instructions

From the primary fabric, cut:
  ★ Four 9½" x 15" panels

From the band fabric, cut:
  ★ Two 5" x 15" panels

From the buckle loop fabric, cut:
  ★ One 3" x 20" strip

# instructions

**1** To make the buckle loops, press under ½" on each long edge of the strip, and then fold the strip in half, wrong sides together. Edgestitch the folded edges. Cut the strip into six 3"-long pieces.

**2** Loop a strip piece through each buckle ring and align the piece ends. Topstitch across the loop close to the ring. Loop the remaining three strip pieces. Position the loop/buckles and empty loops along the side edges of one band panel. Baste the loop ends as shown.

**3** To assemble the pillow front and back, stitch each band panel between two primary panels at their 15"-long edges. (*Note:* On the pillow front, these seams will encase the loop ends.) Stitch the pillow front and back together, matching the band seams at the upper and lower edges, but leave one short edge unstitched.

**4** Trim seams and corners, turn the cover right-side out and press the seams flat. On the pillow front, attach the buckle heads to their loops.

**5** Lightly stuff the cover corners with fiberfill, insert the pillow form, and add more or remove fiberfill as desired. Fold under the seam allowances on the cover open edges and whipstitch the opening closed.

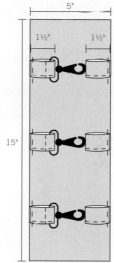

EVENLY SPACE THE LOOPS AND BASTE THEIR ENDS TO THE BAND PANEL EDGES.

2

these easy projects. Throwing a party, hosting a shower, celebrating a birthday or holiday. Whatever the occasion, you can make it sew special with these easy projects.Whatever the occasion, you can make it sew special with these easy projects. Throwing a party, hosting a shower, celebrating a birthday or holiday. Whatever the occasion, you can make it sew special with these easy projects. Throwing a party, hosting a shower, celebrating a birthday or holiday. Whatever the occasion, you can make it sew special with these easy projects. Whatever the occasion, you can make it sew special with these easy projects. Throwing a party, hosting a shower, celebrating a birthday or holiday. Throwing a party, hosting a shower, celebrating

chapter 7

# ideas for easy entertaining

Throwing a party, hosting a shower, celebrating a birthday or holiday. Whatever the occasion, you can make it sew special with these easy projects.

folding chair seat cushion and back slipcover

The folding chair comes in handy for extra seating at parties. Here's an easy way to dress up this basic chair for about $8, using a set of three printed kitchen towels and one purchased cushion insert.

## materials

* ★ 3 print kitchen towels, at least 19" x 25" each
* ★ 15" x 15" x 1" seat cushion insert

## instructions

**1** *To make the cushion cover*, cut one 16" x 16" square from each of the two towels. *Note:* Cut these squares in the towel centers to preserve each towel's hemmed edges (used later as cushion ties).

**2** To make the seat cushion ties, cut four 10"-long strips along the towel hemmed edges, with each strip 1" wider than the hem depth. Press under ½" on one short end of each strip, and then press under ½" twice on each strip long cut edge, to overlap the strip hemmed edge. Edgestitch these folded edges.

**3** Pin the panels together with a pair of ties sandwiched between the layers at two corners, and stitch around three edges and slightly into the fourth edge as shown.

**4** Turn the cover right-side out and insert the cushion through the cover opening. Fold under the seam allowances on the cover open edges and whipstitch them together. Tie the cushion to the chair back braces.

**5** *To make the seat back slipcover*, fold the remaining towel in half widthwise, right sides together, and place it over the chair back. With the towel side edges aligned at the back lower edge, pin-fit the towel around the curve of the chair back, then use tailor's chalk to mark the stitching lines.

**6** Stitch on the marked lines, trim the excess towel, turn right side out and press. Slide the cover over the chair back.

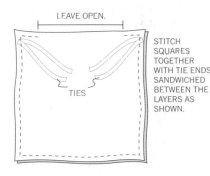

LEAVE OPEN.

STITCH SQUARES TOGETHER WITH TIE ENDS SANDWICHED BETWEEN THE LAYERS AS SHOWN.

TIES

**3**

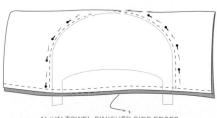

ALIGN TOWEL FINISHED SIDE EDGES.

PIN-FIT THE FOLDED TOWEL TO THE CHAIR BACK.

**5**

baby's bath-time shower gift

Kat[h]

Holly

Ellen

Get your ducks in a row with this baby gift that serves as the shower theme, too ... all inspired by a soft cotton flannel print.

## materials

* 1 yd. 45"-wide white terrycloth fabric
* 1 yd. cotton print flannel fabric featuring ducks
* Bath accessories, such as yellow rubber ducky bath toys, baby shampoo, etc.
* Saucer

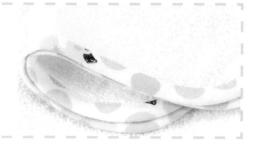

## cutting instructions

From the terrycloth, cut:
* One 36" x 36" towel
* One 10" x 10" washcloth

## instructions

1 Trace around the edge of a saucer and cut on the traced lines to curve all of the towel and washcloth corners.

2 Follow the Cutting and Applying Bias Binding instructions beginning on page 180 to cut 2"-wide bias strips from the flannel and to bind the towel and washcloth edges.

3 Package the completed towel and washcloth with bath accessories to give as a gift.

le that holds "the cake"
l look so much nicer with
ur tablecloth (instead o
ented one). All you need
wire-edge ribbon and sil
we in the bride's colors
roll the ribbon, create
se swag and pinch the
bon at the swag and
e your machine to tack
e pinched ribbon to the
ble th edge. Repeat
swag and tack
bon around the en
loth to Add silk f
each tack by wind
e flower's wire
und the ribbon W
e party's over, take
blec th home and c
e tacks and it's re
the next celebrat
during reception
at holds "the cake"
ok so much nicer with
ur tablecloth (instead o
ented one). All you need
wire-edge ribbon and silk
wers in the bride's colors
roll the ribbon, create a
se swag and pinch the
bon at the swag end

*wedding tablecloth*

The wedding reception table that holds "the cake" will look so much nicer with your tablecloth (instead of a rented one). All you need is wire-edge ribbon and silk flowers in the bride's colors. Unroll the ribbon, create a loose swag and pinch the ribbon at the swag end. Use your machine to tack the pinched ribbon to the tablecloth edge. Repeat to swag and tack the ribbon around the entire tablecloth. Add silk flowers at each tack by winding the flower's wired stem around the ribbon. When the party's over, take your tablecloth home, clip the tacks … and it's ready for the next celebration.

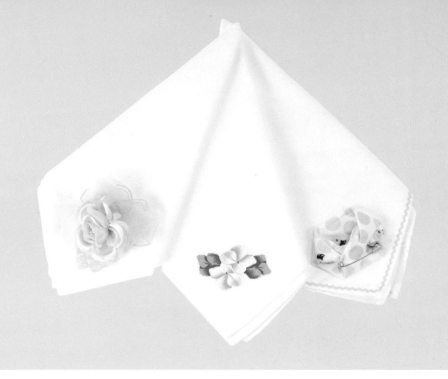

## party napkins

No matter what the occasion or how many people she's serving, Margie always sets her table with cloth napkins. I admire her attitude, which is why I purchased dozens of basic white "hotel" napkins (deeply discounted at a national home products store) for about 50 cents each. This is my stash of party napkins to jazz up with temporary or permanent embellishments! Here are a few napkin ideas to consider for your own party fare:

* *Ribbons & Roses* (left). Tack a length of the same ribbon used to embellish the wedding tablecloth on a napkin corner, and wire the same silk flower or a coordinating floral spray.

* *Floral Appliqué* (center). Apply paper-backed fusible web to the wrong side of a selected fabric motif, then cut it out using very sharp, short-blade scissors. Peel off the paper backing and fuse the motif where desired. Finish the edges with satin stitches.

* *Nanny Napkin* (right). Carry through the party theme, i.e. baby shower, with a fabric embellishment. Cut and sew a double-faced cotton flannel triangle, stitch the open triangle to a napkin corner, then fold it into a diaper shape and secure with a diaper pin. (The hardest part is folding the diaper!)

INTERESTING TRIMS — AND A LITTLE ELASTIC — MAKE EXCELLENT NAPKIN RINGS. (LEFT) TACKING THE ELASTIC ENDS OF A 6"-LENGTH OF THIS FANTASY FLORAL ADDS THE RIGHT "RING" OF FESTIVITY TO A PARTY. (RIGHT) EDGESTITCH A SEAM TAPE CASING TO THE BACK OF FRINGED DENIM TRIM, THREAD ELASTIC CORD THROUGH THE CASING, KNOT THE CORD ENDS, AND YOU'RE DONE! BARBEQUE, ANYONE?

tv tray placemat

Can't get them to come to the table when the big game is on? Bring the table setting to the tray. This placemat with attached silverware/napkin pocket adds a little class to dinner by the glow of television screen.

## materials

* ½ yd. denim or other medium- to heavyweight cotton fabric
* 12" decorative trim (optional)
* Fabric glue (optional)

## cutting instructions

From the denim fabric, cut:
* One 20" x 15" mat
* One 5" x 8" pocket

## instructions

**1** To make the pocket, press under ½" on one 5" edge (lower edge) and both 8" edges (side edges). Press under ½" twice on the remaining 5" edge and topstitch the hem (upper edge). On the pocket lower edge, create two ½"-deep pleats and baste across the pleat folds.

**2** Clean-finish and press under ½" on each placemat edge. Refer to the photo to place the pocket, right-side up, on the placemat, aligning the pocket with the placemat lower left edge corner.

**3** Satin stitch around the placemat and over the pocket left side and lower edges, ⅜" from its folded edge to secure both the placemat hems and attach the pocket to the mat. If desired, glue trim across the pocket upper edge.

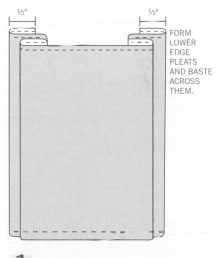

FORM LOWER EDGE PLEATS AND BASTE ACROSS THEM.

½"     ½"

1

## silverware caddy

The silverware pocket on the denim placemat on the previous page can become a standalone silverware/napkin caddy for self-serve buffet entertaining. To make this holder from denim, cut a 10" x 8" panel. Finish one 10" edge with a doubled ½"-deep topstitched hem. Fold the panel in half, right sides together, to measure 5" x 7". Stitch the long edge and across one short end. Turn right-side out and, with the seam centered in back, press the side edges flat. Satin stitch across the lower edge and glue trim around the finished upper edge, if desired.

reversible dining chair cover

When I get tired of the upholstery on my dining room chairs, I change their look with slip-on seat covers. The featured one-piece cover is made from two coordinating silk taffeta prints, but you can opt for less formal fabrics. The covers not only change the look of your good dining chairs, they protect the seat upholstery from spills and stains (helpful when smaller guests are invited to sit at the formal dining table). This is a two-for-one project because the cover is reversible. *Note:* Armless chairs with drop-in upholstered seats are the best candidates for this project.

## materials

* ★ ¾ to 1 yd. of two coordinating 54"-wide decorator fabrics (enough to make two reversible chair covers)
* ★ 1 yd. pattern tracing cloth or muslin
* ★ Low-loft quilt batting
* ★ Corkscrew shaped upholstery pins (optional)

## instructions

**1** To draw the cover pattern, drape the chair seat with pattern tracing cloth or muslin, and trace the seat edges, including the wood frame, if any, surrounding the seat. Pin the cloth lower edges to determine the desired cover length at the front and sides, as well as the back edge flap. *Note:* The figure at right illustrates the seat configuration for this specific chair; your tracing will look different, of course, but you will still follow this pattern-making process.

DESIRED LENGTH

MARK SEAT/FRAME OUTLINE AND DESIRED LENGTH ON PATTERN TRACING CLOTH

DESIRED LENGTH

**1**

PIN, THEN MARK
THE FRONT
CORNER DARTS.

2

**2** Add ½" to the traced edges and cut out the pattern. Place the pattern on the chair seat again and form darts at the front corners to fit the cover over these seat/frame edges. Mark the stitching lines of each dart.

**3** Use the pattern to cut one panel from each fabric and one batting panel. Transfer the corner dart markings to the wrong sides of the fabric panels.

**4** Baste the batting to the wrong side of one panel, and thereafter treat them as a single layer. Stitch the corner darts in each panel, trim the excess dart fabric and press them open.

**5** Pin the panels together and stitch all edges, leaving about 8" unstitched at one edge for turning. Trim the seams, clip the corners, turn right-side out and press the seams flat. Fold under the seam allowances on the open edges and slipstitch the opening closed.

**6** Place the cover on the chair. If desired, secure the cover to the underlying upholstered seat using corkscrew-shaped upholstery pins.

## kids' tablecloth

At some point, the children of the clan graduate and are invited to join their elders at the "big" dining table. Until then, they're usually assigned seats at the "kids' table." Treat your little outcasts like important guests by making a special tablecloth just for them. This 32" x 48" folding table (used for the Game Table Topper project on page 133) needed just 2 yards of 54"-wide decorator fabric for its generously sized cloth. To make a similar cloth, leave the selvage edges as is, finish the cut edges with doubled ½"-deep topstitched hems ... and dinner is served.

# general techniques

Although each project has its own unique instructions, many projects use the same technique(s). Rather than repeating these same instructions and illustrations, I've compiled them here as general techniques, and referred you to specific ones within the project instructions. *Note:* All projects share the Basic Sewing information that appears on pages 175-177. Review this information as you begin your projects to become familiar with these universal terms and techniques.

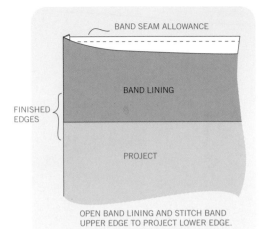

BAND SEAM ALLOWANCE

BAND LINING

FINISHED EDGES

PROJECT

OPEN BAND LINING AND STITCH BAND
UPPER EDGE TO PROJECT LOWER EDGE.

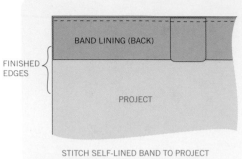

BAND LINING (BACK)

FINISHED EDGES

PROJECT

STITCH SELF-LINED BAND TO PROJECT
LOWER EDGE AND CLEAN-FINISH SEAM.

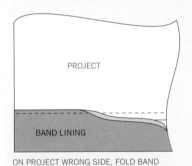

PROJECT

BAND LINING

ON PROJECT WRONG SIDE, FOLD BAND
LINING EDGE OVER STITCHING LINE AND
EDGESTITCH (OR SLIPSTITCH BY HAND).

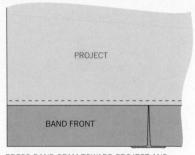

PROJECT

BAND FRONT

PRESS BAND SEAM TOWARD PROJECT AND
TOPSTITCH SEAM.

Bands can be self-lined or lined with another fabric. The Better Ready-Mades on page 108 feature self-lined bands. The Matelassé Coverlet with Zigzag Band on page 80 has a lined band. Once you've sewn the band short side edges, follow the illustration above to stitch the band to the project and finish the lining upper edge.

You can also attach a self-lined band, like the Media Center's pleated skirt and pleated topper bands (see project on page 146). Pin the band double-layer upper edge to the project lower edge, aligning the band/project finished side edges. Stitch the band to the project and clean-finish the seam allowance. Press the seam toward the project and topstitch as shown above.

*basic sewing*

BASTE AND SECURE ONE SET OF BOBBIN THREADS BY WINDING THEM AROUND A STRAIGHT PIN.

DESIRED WIDTH

PULL THE OPPOSITE BOBBIN THREADS TO GATHER THE FABRIC EDGE TO THE DESIRED WIDTH.

gathering

# machine stitches

*Basting*: This long, straight stitch is used to hold fabrics together during fitting and before permanent sewing. It's also used to temporarily hold trim within a seam allowance before the trim edge or header is secured within a seam.

*Edgestitching*: This straight stitch, made quite close to a folded edge, is used to secure hems and attach trims. It can also be used as a substitute for a stitched seam. Edgstitching will show on the right side of the fabric.

*Gathering*: Machine gathering consists of stitching two parallel lines of basting on the fabric right side about ¼" to ⅜" and ½" to ⅝" from its edge. Leave long thread tails at the beginning and end of each basting line. Working from the fabric wrong side, secure one set of bobbin threads around a straight pin, and manually pull the other set to draw up the fabric edge into gathers that reduce the fabric down to the desired width. Evenly distribute the gathers, then secure them with straight stitches in a seam or, for a project like the gathered bed skirt, bind them with double-fold bias tape. After permanently stitching the gathers, clip and remove any basting stitches that show on the fabric right side.

*Staystitching*: This straight stitching is done just inside the seamline to prevent the fabric from stretching out of shape during construction.

*Topstitching*: This straight stitch is done on the right side of a garment or other project, and is often stitched parallel to a folded edge or seam. It can be used for functional purposes (such as securing a hem), decorative purposes, or both.

# hand stitches

*Slipstitch:* This is a nearly invisible stitch formed by inserting the needle into a fold of fabric so that the thread slips under the fold. It can be used to stitch two folded edges together or to join a folded edge to a flat, single layer of fabric (such as a garment hem).

*Whipstitch:* These tiny stitches are taken vertically to join two folded or finished edges of fabric.

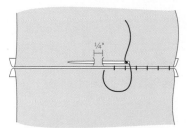

TO JOIN TWO FOLDED EDGES, BRING NEEDLE UNDERNEATH AND THROUGH THE LOWER EDGE FOLD. INSERT THE NEEDLE THROUGH THE UPPER FOLDED EDGE, TAKE A ¼" HORIZONTAL STITCH AND REPEAT.

slipstitch

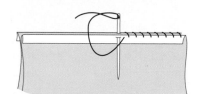

STITCH PERPENDICULAR TO FOLDED EDGES, PICKING UP JUST A FEW FABRIC THREADS AT EACH FOLD WITH EACH STITCH.

whipstitch

STITCH EDGES WRONG SIDES TOGETHER IN A ⅜" SEAM. TRIM SEAM ALLOWANCE TO ¼".

# sewing and finishing seams

*Seam allowances:* Unless otherwise indicated, stitch fabrics right sides together using a ⅝" seam allowance for garment projects, and a ½" seam allowance for all other projects.

*Clean-finished seams:* To prevent raveling, finish seams as you sew them. Common techniques include trimming the seam edges with pinking shears; zigzagging near, but not exactly on, the seam edges; and using an overcast or mock serging stitch (if your machine offers it) to stitch near, but not on, the seam edges.

*French seam:* The French seam encloses the seam edges. To sew a French seam, follow the steps at right. *Note:* The French seam uses a ¾" seam allowance.

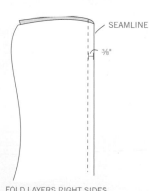

SEAMLINE

⅜"

FOLD LAYERS RIGHT SIDES TOGETHER AROUND SEAM TO ENCLOSE IT; PRESS FLAT. STITCH EDGE AGAIN IN A ⅜" SEAM.

French seam

## box-edge cushion cover

If making a box-edge cushion cover, slide the box band over the cushion edge, centering it on the depth of the original band. Mark a dot, within the seam allowance, at which the band upper and lower edges align with the cushion corners. Also mark the pivot point (for square corners) or the center (for curved corners) of each top/bottom panel corner. With marks aligned, pin the panels to the band edges and stitch, leaving one edge on the lower panel unstitched for turning. *Note:* Clip to the seamline at each band dot for ease in stitching the box-edge corners.

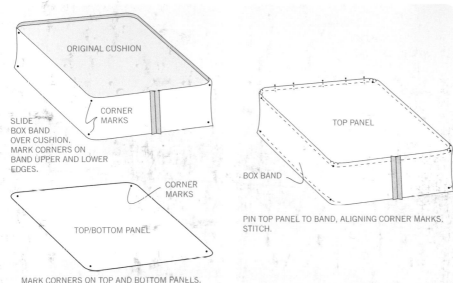

ORIGINAL CUSHION

CORNER MARKS

SLIDE BOX BAND OVER CUSHION. MARK CORNERS ON BAND UPPER AND LOWER EDGES.

CORNER MARKS

TOP/BOTTOM PANEL

MARK CORNERS ON TOP AND BOTTOM PANELS.

TOP PANEL

BOX BAND

PIN TOP PANEL TO BAND, ALIGNING CORNER MARKS. STITCH.

## other covers with box edges

For projects like the Tissue Box Cover on page 71, the Flange Pillow on page 92 and the Monkey Business Toy Chest on page 116, you will join four side panels (or flanges) and stitch them to the corresponding edges of either a top or bottom panel (or, in the case of the flange pillow, the front or back panel). The side panel seams are the pivot points for the box corners. For ease, clip a few seam stitches and spread the seam allowances as shown before stitching each corner.

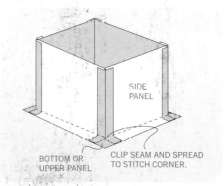

SIDE PANEL

BOTTOM OR UPPER PANEL

CLIP SEAM AND SPREAD TO STITCH CORNER.

**1** Fold the fabric diagonally across its width, press the fold, and cut the fabric on the crease. Place the diagonally-cut edge over a cutting mat with bias/diagonal lines, and use a yardstick and rotary cutter to cut 2"-wide bias strips for ½"-wide bias.

**2** Join the strips, end-to-end as shown, to create the required length of bias for your project, plus 4" to 5" extra.

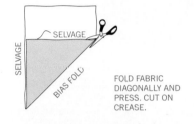

SELVAGE

SELVAGE

BIAS FOLD

FOLD FABRIC
DIAGONALLY AND
PRESS. CUT ON
CREASE.

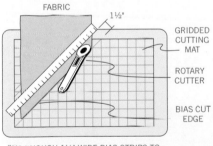

FABRIC

1½"

GRIDDED
CUTTING
MAT

ROTARY
CUTTER

BIAS CUT
EDGE

CUT ENOUGH 1½"-WIDE BIAS STRIPS TO
BIND PROJECT EDGES.

1

⅜"

STITCH STRIP ENDS.

PRESS SEAM OPEN
AND TRIM SEAM
ALLOWANCES AS
SHOWN.

2

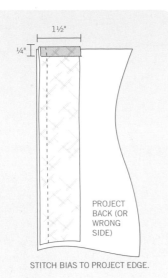

1½"

¼"

PROJECT BACK (OR WRONG SIDE)

STITCH BIAS TO PROJECT EDGE.

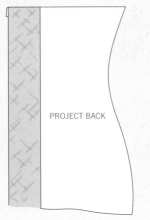

PROJECT BACK

OPEN BIAS AND PRESS SEAM TOWARD IT.

**3**

**3** On the project wrong side (or back), pin the bias strip to the edge. (*Note: For the Growth Chart on page 120, fold under ¼" on each bias end so that it's flush with the chart ends, trimming excess bias as necessary.*) Stitch the bias to the edge using a ⅜" seam. Trim the seam allowance slightly. Open the bias and press the seam toward it.

**4** Press under ⅜" twice on the bias remaining raw edge, folding it over to the project right side to cover the first line of stitching. Edgestitch the bias close to its inner fold.

**5** If joining the bias ends for a continuous bound edge (like the Magazine Caddy on page 145 and the Baby's Bath-Time Shower Gift on page 162), follow the illustration below.

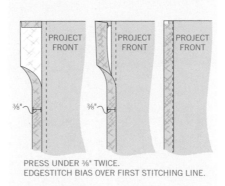

PROJECT FRONT

PROJECT FRONT

PROJECT FRONT

⅜"

⅜"

PRESS UNDER ⅜" TWICE. EDGESTITCH BIAS OVER FIRST STITCHING LINE.

**4**

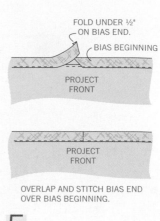

FOLD UNDER ½" ON BIAS END.

BIAS BEGINNING

PROJECT FRONT

PROJECT FRONT

OVERLAP AND STITCH BIAS END OVER BIAS BEGINNING.

**5**

joining curved and straight edges

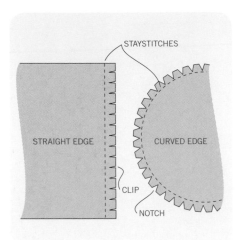

STAYSTITCHES

STRAIGHT EDGE

CURVED EDGE

CLIP

NOTCH

To join a curved edge to a straight one requires edge preparation with notches and clips.

*Notches* are wedges cut from the curved edge, which, when joined to the straight edge, will curve inward. Removing the excess fabric with notches will reduce bulk and help you avoid stitching over an inadvertent fold as you sew the seam. *Clips* are slits cut into the straight edge, which will allow the fabric to spread for easier joining to the curved edge.

Staystitch the curved and straight edges to be joined, then notch and clip each, respectively, up to, but not through, the staystitches. Try to stagger your cuts in each edge so that they are not aligned when you stitch the seam. Cut fewer notches and clips if the fabric is lightweight and loosely woven, and more if the fabric is medium- to heavy-weight.

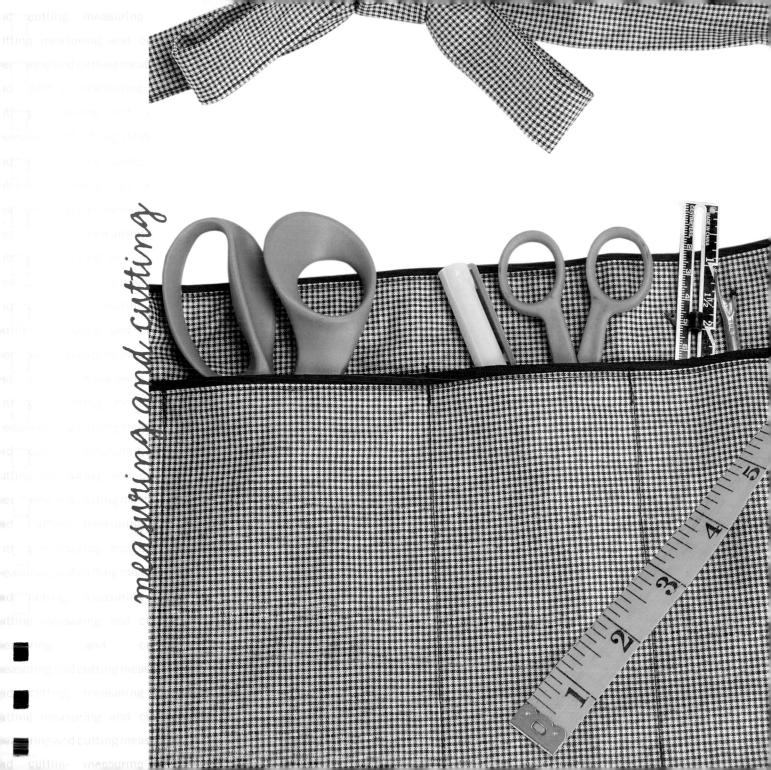

measuring and cutting

# interpreting cutting dimensions

For some projects, specific cutting dimensions are given. Unless otherwise noted, the dimensions should be read as follows:

_____" x _____" means *width x length*

_____" x _____" x ____" means *width x depth x height*

Some cutting dimensions depend on the desired finished size of the project or are determined based on the dimensions of a specific object (examples: a tissue box or a box spring) that the project will cover, thus you will use either "finished size" measurements or object measurements to determine the cutting dimensions. For example, the instructions may state:

"Cut two panels in these dimensions: (width + 2") x (height − 4")"

This means you are to cut a panel equal to the desired finished width (or object width) + 2" by the desired finished height (or object height) − 4". If the width and height are 20" and 30", respectively, you will cut two panels in these dimensions: (20" + 2") x (30" − 4") or 22" x 26". Thus, each cut panel should be 22" wide x 26" long.

# drawing a sample cutting layout

To determine the required yardage for some projects, use the determined cutting dimensions of the project panels and create a sample cutting layout. To do this, first determine whether to draw the layout with the fabric folded or open. *Note:* With garment pattern layouts, the fabric is usually folded in half widthwise, right sides together, and selvages aligned. This layout approach is appropriate if you will be cutting two identical pieces of several panels, such as top/bottom panels for a cushion cover. However, you may be able to conserve yardage by drawing the layout on open fabric, as shown below.

In most cases, you will position panels with their widths running across the fabric width and their lengths parallel to the fabric selvage edge. When the cutting dimensions of a panel exceed the fabric width (such as a box band for a large cushion or the panel for a gathered bed skirt), you will still position the band/panel across the fabric width to conserve yardage in most cases, and cut multiple panels (in the required cutting depth or length) and piece them end to end. *Note:* Remember to add ½" seam allowances to the side edges of partial panels before cutting them.

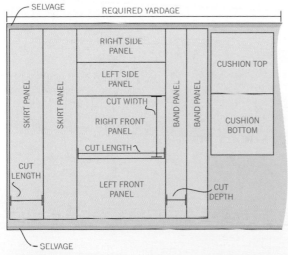

CONSERVE YARDAGE BY BUTTING SQUARE AND RECTANGULAR PANEL EDGES.

## sample layout

# resources

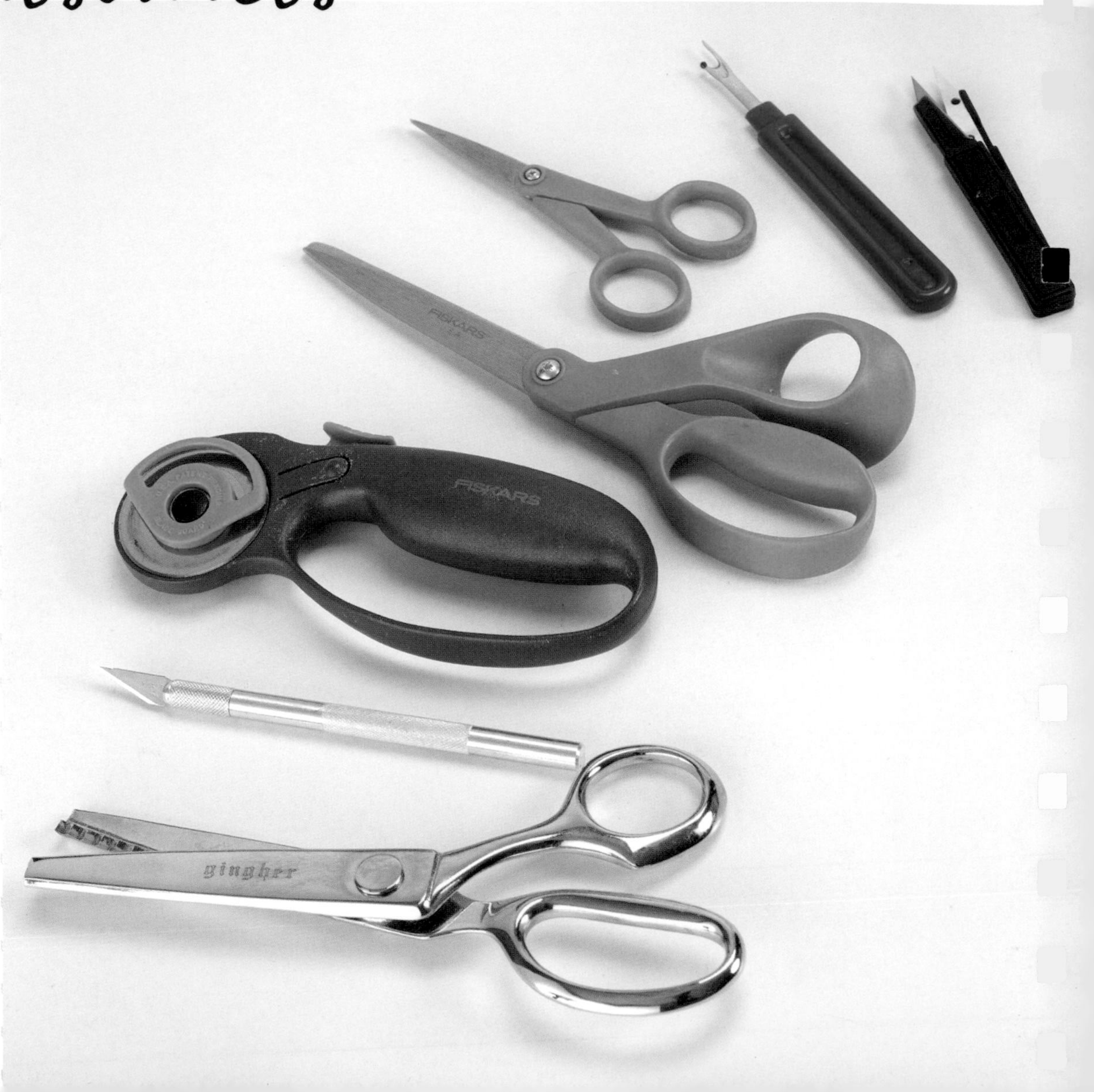

# contributors

The following manufacturers graciously supplied the sewing machine, fabrics and notions used to make many of the projects featured in this book. To find retail and online sources for these products and inquire about others offered by these companies, please visit the company Web sites.

## Bernina® of America

3702 Prairie Lake Ct.

Aurora, IL 60504-6182

www.berninausa.com

*The activa 240 sewing machine (and accessories) used for all projects.*

## Expo International

www.expointl.com

*Fringe, beaded ribbon, gimp braid and other fantasy trims used in the following projects: Flower Pin, Jean Skirt, Tented Canopy, Draped Canopy, Awning Canopy, Monkey Business Toy Chest, Mod Makeovers for Shelf, Café Curtain featured with Pleated Placemat Valance, Floor Pillow, Party Napkins, TV Tray Placemat and Silverware Caddy.*

## Fabric Café

www.fabriccafe.com

*Chenille by the Inch™ trim used for the Growth Chart.*

## Offray

www.offray.com

*Grosgrain, woven and wire-edge ribbons used in the following projects: Tissue Box Cover, Vanity Stool Cushions, Ribbon Shower Curtain, Curtain Ring Scrunchies, Flange Pillow, Media Center, Wedding Tablecloth and Party Napkins.*

## Prym Consumer USA, Inc.

www.dritz.com

*Eyelets and eyelet setting tools, snaps and snap setting tools, and cover button kits and refills used in the following projects: Striped Shower Curtain, Ruffled Shower Curtain, Ribbon Shower Curtain, Quilted Headboard Slipcovers and Magazine Caddy.*

## Sew Creative

4616 N. Prospect Road Unit B

Peoria Heights, IL 61616

www.sewcreative.com

*Machine embroidery stitched on the* Make Me Blush *shelf.*

## Waverly

www.waverly.com

*Decorator fabrics used in the following projects: Matelassé Coverlet with Zigzag Band, T-Shirt Memory Quilt, Quick-Change Layered Bed Skirts, Luxury Linens for Less, Bolster and Flange Pillows, Tent Canopy, Draped Canopy, Awning Canopy, Quilted Headboard Slipcovers, Monkey Business Toy Chest, Growth Chart, Box-Edge Cushion Covers, Rehabbed Ottoman, Magazine Caddy, Media Center and Floor and Accent Pillows.*

## Wrights

www.wrights.com

*Maxi piping and extra-wide double-fold bias tape used in the following projects: Sewer's Tool Belt, Quick-Change Layered Bed Skirts, Luxury Linens for Less and Quilted Headboard Slipcovers (white Matelessé version).*

# other resources

**Baby Lock®**
(800) 422-2953
www.babylock.com

**Brother®**
(800) 422-7684
www.brother.com

**Clotilde®**
P.O. Box 7500
Big Sandy, TX 75755-7500
(800) 772-2891
www.clotilde.com

**Connecting Threads**
P.O. Box 870760
Vancouver, WA 98687-7760
(800) 574-6454
www.connectingthreads.com

**Elna USA**
(800) 848-3562
www.elnausa.com

**Home Sew**
P.O. Box 4099
Bethlehem, PA 18018-0099
(800) 344-4739
www.homesew.com

**Husqvarna® Viking® Sewing Machine Co.**
(800) 358-0001
www.husqvarnaviking.com

**Janome America, Inc.**
(800) 631-0183
www.janome.com

**Keepsake Quilting**
Route 25
P.O. Box 1618
Center Harbor, NH 03226-1618
(800) 438-5464
www.keepsakequilting.com

**Kenmore®**
(800) 349-4358
www.sears.com

**Krause Publications**
(888) 457-2873
www.krause.com

**Nancy's Notions**
333 Beichl Ave.
P.O. Box 683
Beaver Dam, WI 53916-0683
(800) 833-0690
www.nancysnotions.com

**Pfaff**
(800) 997-3233
www.pfaff.com

**Singer®**
(800) 474-6437
www.singerco.com

**Tacony Corp.**
www.tacony.com

**White**
www.whitesewing.com

about the author

about the author

Elizabeth Dubicki, a lifelong sewing enthusiast, is a former staff editor of two national sewing and crafting publications. Today, she's a freelance writer and designer whose work has been published in "Threads," "Sew News," "Creative Machine Embroidery" and Bernina's "Through the Needle" magazines. She co-authored "Decorative Storage" in 2005 (her first Krause Publications book), and is delighted to share her sewing knowledge, experiences and ideas with beginning sewers in this book. "Trust me," she says, "sewing will give you more pleasure and creative rewards than anything you've ever done before!" She resides with her husband in Peoria, Ill., where she's visited (not often enough) by her two grown children.